John Goode has been a writer on food and travel for many years. His interests include natural history, travel, food and wine (both in the cooking and the sampling!), literature and the arts. He lives in Australia.

The Cultured Glutton

A Collection of Culinary Quotes

ranging from the sardonic to the didactic,
the succinct to the sublime,
some in prose, others in rhyme,
designed more to entertain and amuse,
sometimes with wit, often abuse

John Goode

HEADLINE

ISBN 0 7472 3039 0

HEADLINE BOOK PUBLISHING PLC
Headline House
79 Great Titchfield Street
London W1P 7FN

Printed and bound in Great Britain by
Collins, Glasgow

CONTENTS

INTRODUCTION

A writer or speaker often needs an apt *bon mot* that makes a point far more effectively than can be conceived in the time available.

Such pertinent quotes may take the form of a few humorous lines that rhyme, an irate epithet from an individual unhappy with what has been experienced, or just an example of literary style so nicely put that it seems tragic that such a creative phrase should be restricted to its original surroundings.

Eric Quayle, in his book for bibliophiles, *Old Cook Books*, epitomised the last category. No-one with even the slightest interest in food could restrain a wry chuckle after reading his erudite comments on 'Sing a Song of Sixpence'. And how could anyone question the inclusion of such a *rara avis* in this collection?

The same justification can be given for other items, which deal with a subject in its broadest way but not specifically from the culinary viewpoint. Like food well prepared and well presented, a flash of wit is as good as a whiff from the kitchen of a fine chef — and, as such, demands to be shared.

This is unashamedly a selection of gems from people with 'a talent to amuse' — even if the inclusion of one of the items concerning the late Sir Noel Coward was possible only under 'Sartor Resartus'.

In the dipping and tasting, a reader may well find a few items of culinary interest too, for it is no sin to offer the pragmatic if it seems unusual or esoteric.

This is a most subjective selection, offered *sans peur et sans raproche*.

ACKNOWLEDGEMENTS

The isolation of living in Australia is never more manifest than when attempting a compilation of this nature. The task would have been impossible without assistance to go overseas to places where it is possible to locate source material not even housed in Australian libraries.

Such travels were made possible by **Qantas Airways Limited, British Airways**, the **British Tourist Authority** and many other airlines and national tourist organisations who, by making it possible for me to visit so many diverse destinations, indirectly made a major contribution to the preparation of this collection.

Further help was provided by Mrs Ann Tribe (now Stone) of Abigail Books, London, who so patiently searched for copies of rare works on food and associated topics.

Finally, gratitude must be expressed to the staff of the Fisher and Badham Libraries at the University of Sydney who helped in so many ways to make this work possible.

It is to be hoped that all those authors whose work has been cited will forgive the way that their *oeuvres* had to be condensed. This in no way implies that they were in any way guilty of prolixity, but that the strictures of modern publishing impose so tight a discipline on a compiler that the most rigorous editing is unavoidable.

The one consolation is that should readers desire it, there is already a wealth of excellent material on hand to provide a more than substantial foundation for a sequel.

John Goode
Sydney, Australia
June 1986

HUMAN SUSCEPTIBILITIES

ABSTAINER

Ambrose Bierce
1842-c.1914

Abstainer: a weak person who yields to the temptation of denying himself a pleasure.
The Enlarged Devil's Dictionary

Total abstainer: one who abstains from everything but abstention, and especially inactivity in the affairs of others.
Ibid.

ABSTEMIOUSNESS

Benjamin Franklin
1706-90

If, after exercise, we feed sparingly, the digestion will be easy and good, the body lightsome, the temper cheerful, and all the animal functions performed agreeably.
The Art of Procuring Pleasant Dreams

Cicero
106-43 B.C.

Just enough food and drink should be taken to restore our strength and not overburden it.
De Senectute

ABSTINENCE

Herman Melville
1819-91

Better sleep with a sober cannibal than a drunken Christian.
Moby Dick

Sir Thomas Elyot
1490?-1546

Abstinence is whereby a man refraineth from anything which he may lawfully take.
The Governour (1531)

William Watson
1858-1935

And must I wholly banish hence
   These red and golden juices,
And pay my vows to Abstinence,
   That pallidest of Muses?
    To a Fair Maiden Who Bade Me Shun Wine

APHRODISIACS

Thomas Jordan

We'll kiss and be free with Nan, Betty, and Philly,
Have oysters and lobsters and maids by the belly;
Fish-dinners will make a lass spring like a flea,
Dame Venus (Love's goddess) was born of the
   sea.
   With her and with Bacchus we'll tickle the
    sense,
   For we shall be past it a hundred years hence.
   The Epicure (n.d.)

Hans Bazli

After a perfect meal, we are more susceptible to
the ecstasy of love than at any other time . . .
   Cited by Philippa Pullar in *Consuming Passions* (1977)

George Belham

Fish has always been a favourite recommendation
as an aphrodisiac . . . the *oyster* was considered to
be especially stimulating for women on this account. The sea slug, which swells and enlarges
when touched, was popular amongst the Arabs
and Chinese, even when dried and cured . . .
   The Virility Diet, cited by Rydon (n.d.)

John Rydon

Every form, shape and variety of fish, from oysters to eels, has been credited with especial
powers — both in improving performance and
reducing resistance to seduction . . . [However,]
there is no evidence that fishermen are more virile
than landlubbers, and sailors earned their promis-
cuous reputation at a time when they fed mainly
on salt pork and weevil biscuits . . .
   Oysters with Love (1968)

Brillat-Savarin
1755-1826

. . . opinion is unanimous that [fish] are strongly
sexual and awaken in both sexes the instinct for
reproduction . . . These physical truths were without doubt unknown to the ecclesiastical law mak-

ers who imposed a Lenten diet on various priestly orders ... for it is impossible to believe they could deliberately have wished to make even more difficult that vow of chastity already so antisocial in its observances.

Physiologie du Goût

Nicholas Culpeper 1616-54

Peach-tree: ... Venus owns this tree ... the fruit provokes lust.
Asparagus ... being taken fasting several mornings together, stirreth up bodily lust in man or woman, whatever some have written to the contrary.

Complete Herbal

Anonymous

Those who wish to lead virtuous lives should abstain from truffles.

Ancient French proverb

John Goode

The Conquistadores reported that Montezuma insisted on having a large drink of chocolate before entering his harem and it is possible that his insistence on the drink's potential as an aphrodisiac resulted in its continuing popularity at bedtime, although scientists long ago discounted these alleged properties of the cocoa bean.

... green chartreuse does act as a bladder irritant and arouses some women, yet it has never become really trendy in Anglo-Saxon countries, though its cheaper relative, Crème de Menthe, was once the rage in parts of Australia.

'Everyday Narcotics', *Vogue Living* (1981)

Claudia Roden

Sidqi Effendi, in his Turkish cookery manual written in the nineteenth century, gives this recipe for grilling cheese. 'Put a portion of cheese in silver paper. Wrap it up and put it over a fire. When the paper starts to glow the cheese is ready to eat and deliciously creamy ... This is good food which enhances sex for married men.'

The Book of Middle Eastern Food (1968)

APPETITE

Carême
1784-1833

'Sir, my duty is to flatter your appetite, not to regulate it.'
  To King George IV of England

Robert Burns
1759-96

Some hae meat and canna eat,
  And some wad eat that want it,
But we hae meat and we can eat,
  And sae the Lord be thankit.
  The Selkirk Grace

**François
Rabelais**
1494-1553

Appetite comes with eating . . . and thirst departs with drinking.
  Gargantua and Pantagruel

**William
Shakespeare**
1564-1616

. . . who can . . . cloy the hungry edge of appetite
By bare imagination of a feast?
Or wallow naked in December snow
By thinking on fantastic summer's heat?
  Richard II

BELLY

Samuel Johnson
1709-84

Some people have a foolish way of not minding, or pretending not to mind what they eat. For my part, I mind my belly very studiously, and very carefully; for I look upon it, that he who does not mind his belly, will hardly mind anything else.
  Boswell's *Life of Johnson*

George Herbert
1593-1633

The eye is bigger than the belly.
  Jacula Prudentum

**François
Rabelais**
1494-1553

No clock is more regular than the belly.
  Works, IV

Anthony Copley
1567-1607?

Poor men want meat for their stomachs, rich men stomachs for their meat.
  Wits, Fits, etc.

William Penn
1644-1718

The Receipts of Cookery are swelled to a Volume, but a good Stomach excels them all.

Fruits of Solitude

Frederick the Great
1712-86

An army, like a serpent, travels on its belly.

Epigram (also attributed to Napoleon I)

BON VIVEUR

Francis Meynell
1880-¿

A bin of wine, a spice of wit,
A house with lawns enclosing it;
A living river by the door,
A nightingale in the sycamore.

'Bon Viveur' — on Andre Simon, after R. L. Stevenson, used as Introduction to *Art of Good Living*

CALORIES

Frances G. Benedict
1870-¿

The extra calories needed for one hour of intense mental effort would be completely met by the eating of one oyster cracker or one half of a salted peanut.

The Energy Requirements of Intense Mental Effort

CANNIBALISM

Jonathan Swift
1667-1745

I have been assured, by a very knowing American of my acquaintance in London, that a young healthy child well-nursed is at a year old a most delicious, nourishing, and wholesome food, whether stewed, roasted, baked, or boiled, and I make no doubt that it will equally serve in a fricassee, or a ragout.

A Modest Proposal

CHARACTER, EFFECT OF FOOD ON

Sydney Smith
1771-1845

I am convinced that character, talents, virtues and qualities are powerfully affected by beef, mutton, piecrust, and rich soups.

Cited by Tannahill in *The Fine Art of Food*

CONTENTMENT

**Jean Jacques
Rousseau**
1712-78

Happiness: a good bank account, a good cook, and a good digestion.

Attrib.

DEATH AND HOW TO GO

Walter de Map
fl. 1170-1200

Die I must, but let me die drinking in an Inn!
Hold the wine-cup to my lips sparkling from the bin!
So when the angels flutter down to take me from my sin,
'Ah, God have mercy on this sot', the Cherubs will begin.

'The Jovial Priest's Confession' (c.1170)

DELERIUM TREMENS

Oscar Mendelsohn
Psychiatrists state that sufferers from delerium tremens ('the shakes') do not see 'pink elephants'. The delusions are confined to small creatures — spiders and the like.

> 'The Mythology of Beverage Alcohol', *From Cellar and Kitchen* (1968)

DIET AND DIETING

A. B. Cheales
Diet cures more than doctors.

> *Proverbial Folk-lore* (n.d.)

Lady Mary Wortley Montagu 1689-1762
Be plain in dress, and sober in your diet;
In short, my deary! kiss me, and be quiet.

> 'Summary of Lord Lyttelton's Advice'

Anonymous
If doctors fail you, let these three be your doctors: a cheerful mind, rest, and moderate diet.

> *Regimen Sanitatis Salernitanum* (c.1260)

H. S. Leigh 1837-83
If you wish to grow thinner, diminish your dinner,
And take to light claret instead of pale ale;
Look down with utter contempt upon butter,
And never touch bread till its toasted — or stale.

> 'A Day for Wishing'

Angie Dickinson
'Grapefruit juice and young men'.

> Comment, 1985, when asked what kept her so young.

DIGESTION

C. E. Carryl 1841-1920
There's never a question
About my digestion,
Anything does for me!

> *The Plaint of the Camel*

Sydney Smith
1771-1845

I am convinced digestion is the great secret of life.
Letter to Arthur Kinglake, 30 September 1837

William Shakespeare
1564-1616

Things sweet to taste prove in digestion sour.
Richard II

Samuel Butler
1835-1902

The healthy stomach is nothing if not conservative. Few radicals have good digestion.
Notebooks, Mind and Matter: Indigestion

Frère Lorens

Afterwards he wished that he had the neck of a crane and the belly of a cow, that the morsels might remain longer in the throat and be digested more.
Le Somme des Vices et des Vertus (1279)

DRINKERS

Robert Mundle

The colonials [Australians] are here at Cowes . . . their sailing performances have been impressive, their drinking even better.
Comment, 1973

Anonymous

God gave the grape
Good wine to make
To cheer both great and small.
But little fools they drink too much,
And big ones — none at all.
Cited by Walter James in *Antipasto* (1957)

Artemus Ward
1834-67

They drink with impunity, or anybody who invites them.
Moses the Sassy; Programme

Robert Southey
1774-1843

And he thought that all the world over
In vain for a man you might seek,
Who could drink more like a Trojan,
Or talk more like a Greek.
The Devil's Walk

Oscar Wilde
1854-1900

Work is the curse of the drinking classes.
Cited by H. Pearson in *Life of Oscar Wilde*

EATING AND ITS EFFECTS

Alexander Pope
1688-1744

Fame is at best an unperforming cheat;
But 'tis substantial happiness to eat.
Mr D'Urfey's Last Play

Benjamin Disraeli
1804-81

All paradise opens! Let me die eating ortolans to the sound of soft music.
The Young Duke

Erasmus
1465-1536

My heart is Catholic but my stomach Lutheran.
'On his dislike of fish'

Richard Graves
1715-1804

Cloyed with ragouts you scorn my simple food,
And think good eating is man's only good;
I ask no more than temperance can give;
You live to eat, I only eat to live.
Diogenes to Aristippus

Brillat-Savarin
1755-1826

Tell me what you eat and I will tell you what you are.
Physiologie du Goût

Richard Twopeny
1857-1915

... the French eat, the English only feed; we may fairly add that Australians 'grub'.
Town Life in Australia

EPICURE

A. J. A. Symons

The epicure is not a man who thinks of, and lives for, his belly alone; he is not a sensualist for whom dinner is merely an elaborate prelude to sexual passion; he is not a hedonist who sees life as a succession of pleasurable sensations obtained by hook, crook, or levitation ... He is simply one who cultivates a refined taste for the pleasures of the table ...

Introduction to *The Epicure's Anthology*, compiled by Nancy Quennell (n.d.)

EPICUREANISM

Sydney Smith
1771-1845

Man could direct his ways by plain reason and support his life by tasteless food; but God has given us wit, and flavour, and brightness and laughter . . .

Dangers and Advantages of Wit

Baroness Orczy
1865-1947

. . . the Englishman lives like a king and eats like a pig, and the Hungarian lives like a pig, but God knows, he eats like a king.

Reply to someone who asked her to compare the two countries; cited by George Lang in *The Cuisine of Hungary* (1971)

Andrea Trevisano
fl. 1497

. . . the English being great epicures, and very avaricious by nature, indulge in the most delicate fare themselves and give their household the coarsest bread and beer, and cold meat baked on Sunday for the week. . . .

Cited by Philippa Pullar in *Consuming Passions*

EXCESS

John Selden
1584-1654

'Tis not the eating, nor 'tis not the drinking that is to be blamed, but the excess.

Table Talk

FOOD AND DRINK

Frank Muir

Such has been the importance of food to the human race, both as a source of pleasure and as fuel, that almost everything we eat or drink has at some time or other been denounced as illegal, immoral, irreligious, dangerous or nasty.

The Frank Muir Book (1976)

G. Bernard Shaw
1856-1950

There is no love sincerer than the love of food.

Man and Superman

Ogden Nash 1902-71	Some singers sing of women's eyes, And some of women's lips . . . Yet I, though custom call me crude, Prefer to sing in praise of food. 'The Clean Platter' in *The Face is Familiar* (1954)
	By undraped nymphs I am not wooed; I'd rather painters painted food . . . Ibid.
Oswald Burdett	All foods, from Cornish mackerel to American shaddocks (and, indeed, especially fruit) taste so much better in the place of their origin. *A Little Book of Cheese* (1935)
Frank Harris 1855-1931	. . . while the desire for food is necessary and dominant, it has very little to do with the higher nature, with the mind or the soul; whereas the sex-urge is connected with everything sweet and noble in the personality . . . *My Life and Loves*
Australian Aborigines	To make good food go farther, eat less. Attrib.
Molière 1622-73	I live on good food, not fine words. *Les Femmes Savantes*

FOOD AND ROMANCE

Fanny Fern 1811-72	The way to a man's heart is through his stomach. *Willis Parton*
Jocasta Innes	Almost all men . . . can be appeased by platefuls of hot and fiery food — curry, or hotter still, Chilli con Carne. You must provide plenty of cold beer or lager to wash them down with. *The Pauper's Cookbook* (1971)

FOOD AND TEMPERAMENT

Anonymous   The foods that are dear to men of the goodness-mood are moist, oily, firm, and cordial ... The foods that are dear to men of fieriness are bitter, sour and salty ...

Bhagavad-gita

FOOD AS A CHARACTER INDICATION

Colette
1873-1954   If I had a son who was ready to marry, I would tell him, 'Beware of girls who don't like wine, truffles, cheese, or music'.

Cited by Evan Jones in *The Book of Cheese*

FOOD AS WAGES

Reay Tannahill   'Number of breads' became a measure of wealth, and for hundreds of years wages were paid in bread and beer. A peasant [in ancient Egypt] might be paid three breads and two jugs of beer daily, while an important official would receive an annual salary of 900 fine wheat breads, 36,000 flat breads, and 360 jugs of beer.

The Fine Art of Food (1968)

GLUTTONY

Charpentier   Diamond Jim Brady [a railroad magnate] came regularly ... I think no zoo could afford to keep such a magnificent appetite ... For dinner he would have two portions of melon, two plates of soup, a whole sea of bass, mushrooms, a complete duck, three vegetables and three desserts. He swallowed orange juice a half a pint at a gulp ... I tell you, he was as voracious for the last mouthful as for the first.

Those Rich and Great Ones (1935)

Samuel Johnson
1709-84   If once you find a woman gluttonous, expect from her very little virtue.

Letter, 1783

Edward Ward
1667-1731

Then all went to work, with such rending and
  tearing
Like a kennel of hounds on a Quarter of Carrin,
When done with the Flesh, they claw'd off the
  Fish
With one Hand at Mouth, and th'other in th'dish.

'City Feet', cited by Pullar in *Consuming Passions*

Anonymous

A young man, about nineteen . . . ate a leg of pork
of six pounds weight, and a pease-pudding weigh-
ing in proportion, at a public house in Islington,
for a trifling wager, in less than three-quarters of
an hour; after which he drank a pint of brandy off,
at two draughts, and went away, seemingly in
perfect health.

Annual Register (1766)

Leon de Fos

For the man who would eat like a glutton,
A good stomach is worth more than mutton,
For what use is the best
If you cannot digest,
And your teeth are exceedingly rotten.

'Gastronomia'

Alexander Pope
1688-1744

When the tired glutton labours thro' a treat
He finds no relish in the sweetest meat;
He calls for something bitter, something sour,
And the rich feast concludes extremely poor.

Imitations of Horace: Satires

Frank Harris
1855-1931

Self-indulgence in eating and drinking is simply
loathsome and disgusting to all higher natures,
and yet it is persisted in by the majority of mankind without let or hindrance. What preacher ever
dares to hold the fat members of his congregation
up to ridicule, or dreams of telling them that they
are not only disgusting but stupidly immoral and
bent on suicide.

My Life and Loves

**Patricius, Bishop
of Gaeta**

Gluttony kills more than the sword.

Cited in George Herbert's *Jacula Prudentum* (c.1620)

Reay Tannahill

. . . in 1577, the Venetian ambassador to Paris
could not bring himself to enthuse about French

food. The people, he reported, were quite immoderate, eating four or five times a day as and when they felt inclined, consuming very little bread or fruit but a great deal of meat ... They 'ruin their stomachs and bowels by eating too much, as the Germans and Poles do by drinking too much'.

Citing Girolamo Lippomano's *Viaggio* (1577), in *Food in History* (1973)

GOURMET

**Antonia
Williams**

Richard II was the first gourmet king [of England]
'Dinner Party, Then and Now', *Vogue* (1979)

HAIR OF THE DOG

John Heywood
c.1497-c.1580

I pray thee let me and my fellows have
A hair of the dog that bit us last night.
Proverbs

Anonymous

In mediaeval times, if you were bitten by a dog and burnt some of its hairs, you were said to avoid rabies — what alchemists described as *simila similibus curantur*.
Not known

HANGOVER CURES

Sir Hugh Platt

Drink first a good large draught of salad oil, for that will float upon the wine which you shall drink, and suppress the spirits from ascending into the brain. Also, what quantity soever of new milk you drink first, you may well drink thrice as much wine after, without danger of being drunk. But how sick you shall be with this prevention, I will not here determine.
Cited by Tannahill *The Fine Art of Food* (1968)

**William
Shakespeare**
1564-1616

Will the cold brook, candied with ice, caudle thy morning taste, to cure thy o'-er-night's surfeit.
Timon of Athens

John Goode and Carol Willson   Some Americans swear by the prairie oyster . . . an unbroken egg yolk on top of which you pour, well mixed, a good pinch of salt, a teaspoon each of tomato ketchup, Worcestershire sauce and lemon juice, half a teaspoon of vinegar, a drop of tabasco and a good pinch of cayenne. Instructions read:

'Shut eyes, open mouth,
Murmur prayers for the soul,
Pop in and swallow whole'.

Revolting! It sounds more like an ancient Roman emetic or a means of exorcising a devil . . .

'Hair of the Dog or Prairie Oyster: Name Your Antidote', *Sydney Morning Herald*, 12 October 1982

HANGOVERS

George Ade
1866-1944

A dark brown taste, a burning thirst,
A head that's ready to split and burst.

'Remorse', from *The Sultan of Sulu*

Rudyard Kipling
1865-1936

I've a head like a concertina: I've a tongue like a button stick.
Cells

HEALTH

François Rabelais
c.1494-1553

Rise at five, dine at nine; sup at five, to bed at nine.
Works

Anonymous

When the Englishman's liver is brown and good
He has tea, tobacco and ale.
When the Englishman's liver is green and bad
He will pine and tell no tale.
Cited in *We Shall Eat and Drink Again* (c.1943)

HUNGER

Charles Lamb
1775-1834

I came home, hungry as a hunter.
Letter to Coleridge, April 1800

| **New Testament** | I was an hungred, and ye gave me meat: I was thirsty, and ye gave me drink . . . |
| | *St Matthew* |

| **John Heywood** c.1497-c.1580 | Hunger makes hard beans sweet. |
| | *Proverbs* |

| **Albert Einstein** 1879-1955 | An empty stomach is not a good political adviser. |
| | Cited by M. F. K. Fisher in *Physiology of Taste* |

| **W. H. Auden** 1907-73 | Hunger allows no choice To the citizen or to the police; We must love one another or die. |
| | *September 1, 1939* |

| **Anonymous** | Ten pounds of flour, ten pounds of beef, some sugar and some tea, That's all they give to a hungry man, until the Seventh Day. If you don't be moighty sparing, you'll go with a hungry gut . . . |
| | 'The Old Bark Hut' (early Australian bush song that commented on rations provided by outback station owners) |

INDIGESTION

| **Philip Edward Muskett** 1857-1909 | . . . the curse of the land [Australia] — dyspepsia — brought on in a great measure by badly cooked and therefore indigestible food. |
| | *The Art of Living in Australia* (1894) |

INTOXICATION

| **Mauduit** | Intoxication . . . embraces five stages: jocose, bellicose, lachrymose, comatose, and morotose. |
| | *The Vicomte in the Kitchen* (1933) |

| **G. K. Chesterton** 1874-1936 | Before the Roman came to Rye or to the Severn strode, The rolling English drunkard made the rolling English road. |
| | 'The Rolling English Road' |

W. R. Alger
1822-1905

Beware the deadly fumes of that insane elation
Which rises from the cup of mad impiety,
And go, get drunk with that divine intoxication
Which is more sober far than all sobriety.

'The Sober Drunkenness', *Oriental Poetry*

John Singleton

The advertising industry lives a very cyclical sort
of life. December is the month for getting pissed.

Comment, 1974

B. H. Burt
1876-?

One evening in October,
when I was far from sober,
And dragging home a load with manly pride,
My feet began to stutter,
So I laid down in the gutter,
And a pig came up and parked right by my
side . . .
Till a lady passing by was heard to say:
'You can tell a man who boozes
By the company he chooses'.
Then the pig got up and slowly walked away.

'Once a Clown, Always a Clown'

R. W. Emerson
1803-82

The secret of drunkenness is that it insulates us in
thought, while it unites us in feeling.

Quoting George R. in *Journal* (1857)

Anonymous

Intoxication is forbidden upon pain of death . . .
to men and women alike, yet those who had
reached the age of seventy years, provided they
had children and grandchildren, were exempt
from this prohibition.

Aztec *Codex Mendoza*

Richard Porson
1759-1808

I went to Strasburg, where I got drunk
With that most learn'd Professor Brunk;
I went to Wortz, where I got drunken,
With that more learn'd Professor Ruhnken.

'On a German Tour'

Robert Herrick
1591-1674

Born I was to be old,
And for to die here.
After that, in the mould
Long for to lye here.
But before that day comes,

Still I be Bousing*
For I know, in the Tombe
There's no Carousing.
'Anacreontike'
* boozing

Thomas Peacock
1785-1866

Not drunk is he, who from the floor
Can rise alone, and still drink more;
But drunk is he who prostrate lies,
Without the power to drink or rise.
The Misfortune of Elphin

Confucius
c.551-478 B.C.

When the guests have drunk too much,
They shout out and brawl.
They disorder the dishes;
They keep dancing in a fantastic manner.
Thus when they have drunk too much
They become insensible to their errors . . .
Drinking is a good institution
Only when there is good deportment in it.
Chih Ching ['Book of Songs']

Jonathan Swift
1667-1745

Much drinking, little thinking.
Letter to Stella, 26 February 1711

Old Testament

Look not, thou, upon the wine when it is red,
When it giveth his colour in the cup . . .
At the last it biteth like a serpent,
And stingeth like an adder.
Proverbs

R. H. Barham
1788-1845

She pledged him once, and she pledged him
twice,
And she drank as a lady ought not to drink.
'A Lay of Saint Nicholas'

Anonymous

Stocks, with comfortable accommodation for five
couples of ladies and gentlemen who cannot pay
the usual fines for indulging at the shrine of Bacchus, have been erected at the corner of Bathurst
Street. They are accompanied by a whipping post,
and have a fine appearance. They are quite an
addition to the Scot's Church, which is nearly
completed.
'Stocks for Ladies', *Sydney Gazette*(1835)

| **Kenneth Tynan**
1927-80 | What, when drunk, one sees in other women, one sees in Garbo sober. |
| | <div align="right">Cited in Halliwell's *Filmgoer's Book of Quotes*</div> |

MINERAL WATER

Anonymous	Here lie I and my four daughters, Killed by drinking Cheltenham waters, Had we but stuck to Epsom Salts We wouldn't have been in these here vaults.
	'Cheltenham Waters'
Anonymous	Here lies the body of Mary Ann Lowder, She burst while drinking a Seidlitz powder. Called from this world to her heavenly rest, She should have waited till it effervesced.
	'Mary Ann Lowder'

MODERATION

John Heywood c.1497-c.1580	Enough is as good as a feast.
	Proverbs. Also used by Chapman (*Eastward Hoe*), Vanbrugh (*The Relapse*), Bickerstaff (*Love in a Village*), and others
La Rochefoucauld 1613-80	Moderation is like sobriety: one would like to eat more, but one fears to make oneself ill.
	Maximes
Oscar Wilde 1854-1900	Moderation is a fatal thing, Lady Hunstanton. Nothing succeeds like excess.
	A Woman of No Importance

MORNING AFTER

| **George Ade**
1866-1944 | The water wagon is the place for me
At twelve o'clock I felt immense,
Today I favour total abstinence.
My eyes are bleared, and red, and hot,
I ought to eat but I cannot; |

It's no time for mirth and laughter —
The cold grey dawn of the morning after.

'Remorse', in *The Sultan of Sulu*

Cyril Ray

So, if prevention is our aim, let us remember the young lady who shyly asked her doctor for an infallible method of contraception. 'Nothing could be simpler', he said, 'just a glass of cold water, my dear'.

The lady was surprised . . .

'But do tell me,' she said: 'is it to be taken, er — before, or — ahem — after? It could hardly' she blushed 'be taken during . . .'

'No, no,' said the doctor: 'Instead of . . .'

Cited in *The Complete Book of Spirits and Liqueurs* (1977)

Anonymous

The glances over cocktails
That seemed to be so sweet
Don't seem quite so amorous
Over the Shredded Wheat.

'Wine, Women and Wedding'

NOBLESSE OBLIGE

Cole Lesley

Noel wrote in his journal: 'The hubbub about the Queen Mother coming to lunch with me . . . is the talk of the island . . .'

Drama set in over the lobster mousse which . . . was of an unlovely grey and frozen hard as iron. To my suggestion that it should be placed on a chair in the sun to defreeze, Mae the cook shrieked, 'You can't do that, the cats will get at it!' . . . Noel at one point reported it had reached the consistency of an ordinary Slazenger tennis ball. By the time I made one last despairing visit . . . the mousse had begun to melt and my thumb went clean through it. Noel now assumed an air of authority . . . He made some delicious iced green-pea soup in the blender, spiked with fresh mint from the garden. '. . . Lunch was a great success . . . introduced the Queen Mother to Bullshots, she had two and was delighted . . .'

The Life of Noel Coward (1978)

PROHIBITION

John B.
Goodwin
Prohibition will work great injury to the cause of temperance. It is a species of intemperance within itself, for it goes beyond the bounds of reason, in that it attempts to control a man's appetite by legislation and makes a crime out of things that are not crimes.

> This was wrongly attributed to Abraham Lincoln in *Wet Slanders of Abraham Lincoln* (1887)

STOMACH

Charles Lamb
1775-1834
He hath a fair sepulchre in the grateful stomach of the judicious epicure — and for such a tomb might be content to die.

> 'Dissertation upon Roast Pig' *Essays of Elia*

Jerome K.
Jerome
1859-1927
Who invented that mischievous falsehood that the way to a man's heart was through his stomach? How many a silly woman, taking it for truth, has let love slip out of the parlour while she was busy in the kitchen? Of course, if you were foolish enough to marry a pig ... A moderately cooked dinner — let us say a not-too-well cooked dinner, with you looking your best ... makes a pleasanter meal for us, after the day's work is done, than that same dinner, cooked to perfection, with you silent, jaded, and anxious, your pretty hair untidy, your pretty face wrinkled with care concerning the sole, with anxiety regarding the omelette.

> *The Second Thoughts of an Idle Fellow* (1898)

Voltaire
1694-1778
Thought depends absolutely on the stomach, but in spite of that, those who have the best stomachs are not the best thinkers.

> Letter to d'Alembert, 20 August 1770

'... STUFF AS DREAMS ARE MADE ON ...'

Gareth Powell
When I go to Heaven I want to be in an English pub, which has been stocked by an American

landlord with a Rubenesque barmaid in floury
skin and black satin, and I will be drinking cold
Australian beer.

'There are No Good Pubs in Australia', *Sydney Morning Herald* (1985)

TASTE

de Montaigne
1533-92

Chacun à son goût [Each to his own taste].
Old French proverb, quoted in *Essays*

Alexander Pope
1688-1744

Talk what you will of taste, my friend, you'll find
Two of a face as soon as of a mind.
Imitations of Horace

Jeremy Taylor
1613-67

De gustibus non est disputandum [There is no disputing about taste].
Latin proverb, quoted in *Reflections upon Ridicule*

R. L. Stevenson
1850-94

I have always suspected public taste to be a mongrel product, out of affectation by dogmatism.
Virginibus Puerisque

TEMPERANCE

Anonymous

Beer is Best — Left Alone
Temperance advertisement, cited by Michael Green
in *The Art of Coarse Drinking* (1973)

Anonymous

Here's to a temperance supper,
With water in glasses tall,
And coffee and tea to end with —
And me not there at all!
A toast

John Milton
1608-74

If all the world
Should in a pet of temperance feed on pulse,
Drink the clear stream, and nothing wear but
freize . . .
And we should serve him as a grudging
master, . . .
And live like Nature's bastards, not her sons.
Comus

THIRST

Anonymous

He who is master of his thirst is master of his health.

> Old French proverb

Edna St Vincent Millay
1892-1950

I drank at every vine.
The last was like the first,
I came upon no wine
So wonderful as thirst.

> *Feast*

Rudyard Kipling
1865-1936

Ship me somewhere east of Suez, where the best is like the worst,
Where there aren't no Ten commandments an' a man can raise a thirst.

> 'Mandalay'

Cervantes
1547-1616

'If I had a water thirst', replied Sancho, 'there are wells on the road where I could have quenched it'.

> *Don Quixote*

Rachel Henning
1826-1914

You never know what thirst is unless you have travelled a whole day under an Australian sun without water.

> *The Letters of Rachel Henning* (1862)

WELL BEING

Christopher Morley
1890-1957

Benign with Burgundy and cheese souffle . . .

> *Translations from the Chinese*

WOMAN'S WORK

Anonymous

A Woman's Work is Never Done.

> Title of English 17th century ballad

Théodore de Banville
1823-91

You, you do everything, the washing and baking,
All with a light hand, never quaking,
You know, too, how to preserve citrons . . .

> 'To His Wife', cited in *Feasts of a Militant Gastronome*

Epitaph in Bushey churchyard

Here lies a poor woman who always was tired,
For she lived in a place where help wasn't hired.
Her last words on earth were, 'Dear friends I am
    going
Where washing ain't done, nor sweeping, nor
    sewing,
And everything there is exact to my wishes
For there they don't eat and there's no washing
    dishes . . .'

Quoted in letter to *Spectator* (1922)

BARLEY'S BEST

BEER AND ALE

Alexis Lichine   Ale: a kind of beer, formerly made without hops
and drunk fresh.
Encyclopedia of Wines and Spirits (1975)

THE DIFFERENCE

John Gerrard   The manifest vertues in Hops do manifestly argue
the holesomeness of Beere above all; for the hops
rather make it a Physicall drinke to keep the body
in health.
Herbal (1597)

ACQUIRING THE TASTE

G. Bernard Shaw   I don't like beer.
1856-1950   *Candida III*

Cyril Pearl   If you carry out a blindfold test . . . you'll find that
the beer snob is just as much a galah as the wine
snob.
Beer, Glorious Beer (1969)

A. E. Housman   Say, for what were hopyards meant,
1859-1936   Or why was Burton built on Trent?
Oh many a peer of England brews
Livelier liquor than the muse,
And malt does more than Milton can
To justify God's ways to man.
Ale, man, ale's the stuff to drink
For fellows whom it hurts to think:
Look into the pewter pot
To see the world as the world's not.
A Shropshire Lad

**George
Farquhar**
1678-1707

I have fed purely upon ale; I have eat my ale, drank my ale, and I always sleep upon ale.

The Beaux' Stratagem

HISTORICAL

Athenaeus
fl. c.200

Those who drank [Egyptian] beer were so pleased with it that they sang and danced, and did everything like men drunk with wine. Now Aristotle says that men who are drunk with wine show it in their faces; but those who have drunk too much beer, fall back and go to sleep; for wine is stimulating, but beer has a tendency to stupefy.

Cited by Tannahill in *Fine Art of Food*

Reay Tannahill

In Sumer, eight types of barley beer seem to have been made, another eight from an early type of wheat, and three from mixed grains . . . The Code of Hammurabi . . . before 1750 B.C. . . . condemns ale-houses and their under-strength, over-priced beer.

Citing Isaac Myer's *Oldest Books in the World* (1900), in *Food in History* (1973)

John Aubrey
1626-97

Greeke, Heresie, Turkey-cocks, and Beere,
Came into England all in a year.

Brief Lives (c.1680)

Philip G. King
1758-1808

The raising and supplying of barley will greatly depend on the settlers, in exchange for which they are assured of beer.

Governor's Order, 1 October 1804

Anonymous

The art of brewing, as has been well remarked by Cobbett, is very similar to the process of making tea.

Magazine of Domestic Economy (1837)

Sydney Smith
1771-1845

What two ideas are more inseparable than beer and Britannia? — what event more awfully important to an English colony, than the erection of the first brewhouse?

Edinburgh Review (1823)

33

RESPONSES

Thomas Peacock
1785-1866

The rich man has a cellar,
And a ready butler by him;
The poor must steer
For his pint of beer
Where the saints can't choose to spy him.
Rich and Poor

Anonymous

A parson who had the remarkable foible
Of minding the bottle more than the Bible,
Was deemed by his neighbours to be less
perplex'd
In handling a tankard than handling a text.
The Parson

Calverley
1831-84

Life is with such all beer and skittles;
They are difficult to please about their victuals.
Contentment

Alexander Pope
1688-1744

Flow, Welsted, flow
Like thine inspirer, Beer,
Tho' stale, not ripe; tho' thin, yet never clear;
So sweetly mawkish, and so smoothly dull;
Heady, not strong, and foaming tho' not full.
The Dunciad

Gareth Powell

Australian beer is one of Australia's national
treasures. When the managing director of Fosters
compared its taste to being kissed on the tongue
by an angel, he was erring on the side of
conservatism.
'There Are No Good Pubs in Australia', *Sydney Morning Herald*, 19 December 1985

HAIL FELLOW . . .

John Gay
1688-1732

Give me a bumper, fill it up:
See how it sparkles in the cup;
Oh how shall I regale!
Can any taste this drink divine,
And then compare rum, brandy, wine,
Or aught with happy Ale?
A Ballad on Ale

Anonymous	Beer, beer, glorious beer!
	Fill yourselves right up to here!
	Drink a good deal of it,
	Make a good meal of it,
	Stick to your old-fashioned beer!
	Don't be afraid of it,
	Drink till you're made of it,
	Now altogether, a cheer!
	Up with the sale of it,
	Down with the pail of it,
	Glorious, glorious beer!

> Late 19th century music-hall song

OWT IS BETTER THAN NOWT

Alcuin 735-804	But woe is me. There is death in the pot. O man of God. The wine is gone from our wineskins and bitter beer rageth in our bellies.

> *Epistles* (c.800)

'Dryblower' **Murphy**	I do not whine as others may Of money I've misused; Ah no, I only think today Of pints that I've refused . . .

> 'Pints That I've Refused', *Bulletin*

'Slim Dusty' 1926-	It's lonesome away from your kindred and all, By the campfire at night, where wild dingoes call, But there's nothing so lonesome, so morbid or drear, Than to stand in the bar of a pub with no beer. Then the Swaggie comes in smother'd in dust and flies, He throws down his roll, rubs the sweat from his eyes, But when he is told, he says, 'What's this I hear? I've trudged fifty flamin' miles to a pub with no beer!'

> 'A Pub With No Beer' (popular Australian song)

BEASTLY ASSOCIATIONS

Thomas Hood 1799-1845	Hundreds of men were turned into beasts, Like the guests of Circe's horrible feasts, By the magic of ale and *cider*.

> *Miss Kilmansegg: Her Birth*

| James Woodforde | Brewed a vessel of strong Beer ... My two large Piggs, by drinking some Beer grounds ... got so amazingly drunk by it, that they were not able to stand and appeared like dead things almost.
Diary of a Country Parson, 1758-1802 |

RETRIBUTION

| E. Cunningham Dax | There aren't many countries of the world where people get the DTs on beer. Australia is one of them.
Comment, 1969 |

| Anonymous medical columnist | People who drink beer by the gallon ... terrible things go on in their stomachs while they sleep. And their sex life is equally terrible.
Sun , Sydney (1970) |

AS A BRIBE

| William Blake 1757-1827 | But if the Church would give us some ale,
And a pleasant fire our souls to regale,
We'd sing and we'd pray all the livelong day
Nor ever once wish from the Church to stray.
'The Little Vagabond', *Songs of Experience* |

SIC TRANSIT . . .

| Anonymous | Here sleeps in peace a Hampshire grenadier.
Who caught his death by drinking cold small beer;
Soldiers, take heed from his untimely fall,
And when you're hot, drink strong, or not at all.
Epitaph at Winchester, England (1764) |

| Anonymous | Here John Randall Lies,
Who counting of his Tale,
Lived threescore years and Ten
Such vertue was in ale.
Cited by John Watney in Peter Owen, *Beer is Best* (1974) |

| | Ale was his meat,
Ale was his drink,
Ale did his heart revive.
And if he could have drunk his ale,
He still had been alive.
Ibid. |

Anonymous

Hail, hail to thee Blythe spirit,
Wherever you may be,
A drinking man of merit
When grog was flowing free.
(Green were New England's pastures
And brown the foaming ale,
At tippling they were masters
in Old-time Armidale).
The glass you raised is broken,
The slate wiped clean at last;
But your embottled token
Revives the groggy past.
Death, as you wrote, is certain,
'Time, gents!', the Reaper calls,
But we, this side the curtain,
Salute you ere it falls,
And smile at your confessions
Of dozens downed in glee,
Dead Clerk of Petty Sessions,
Blythe Spirit, hail to thee!

To Sydney Blythe, Clerk of Petty Sessions (1870),
cited by Cyril Pearl in *Beer Glorious Beer* (1969)

Anonymous

She drank good ale, good punch and wine
And lived to the age of ninety-nine.

Rebecca Freeland at Edwallon, Notts., 1741, cited in
Rowland Watson, *Merry Gentlemen*

Anonymous

'Twas as she tript from Cask to Cask,
In at a bung hole quickly fell,
Suffocation was her task,
She had no time to say farewell.

Ann Collins at King Stanley, Glos., 1804, Ibid.

Lord Byron
1788-1824

John Adams lies here, of the parish of Southwell,
A carrier who carried his can to his mouth so well;
He carried so much, and he carried so fast,
He could carry no more — so was carried at last;
For the liquor he drunk, being too much for one,
He could not carry-off — so he's now carried-on.

To John Adams, carrier, of Southwell

IT PAYS TO ADVERTISE

**Henry
d'Avranches**

For muddy, foggy, fulsome, puddle stinking,
For all of these, Ale is the only drinking.

Cited by John Taylor (1637)

Anonymous	Ne'er tell me of liquors from Spain or from France, They may get in your heels and inspire me to dance, But ale of old Burton if mellow and right Will get in your head and inspire you to fight. *In Praise of Burton Ale*
C. S. Calverley 1831-84	O Beer! Oh Hodgson, Guinness, Allsop, Bass! Names that should be on every infant's tongue. *Beer*
Anonymous	Twice the man on Worthington. *Advertisement in a Leicestershire pub*

GUINESS' STOUT

Fergus Allen	The Garden of Eden (described in the Bible) Was Guiness's Brewery (mentioned by Joyce) Where innocent Adam and Eve were created And dwelt from necessity rather than choice;
	For nothing existed but Guiness's Brewery, Guiness's Brewery occupied all, Guiness's Brewery, everywhere, anywhere — Woe that expulsion succeeded the fall! . . .
	The anger and rage of the Lord were appalling, He wrathfully cursed them for taking to drink And hounded them out of the brewery, followed By beetles (magenta) and elephants (pink). *Untitled verse, Yet More Comic and Curious Verse*
Walter James	Guiness once advertised that their product was an excellent *cholagogue* — something which stimulates the liver and increases the flow of bile . . . Stout is simply a dark beer, getting its colour from extra-roasting of the malt and much of its quality from the water used for fermentation. *Antipasto (1957)*

MALT

Anonymous	Wha hes gud malt and makis ill drink, Wa mot be hir werd!

I pray to God scho rot and stink,
Sevin yeir abone the erd

     Cited by G. F. Maine in *A Book of Scotland*

PORTER

Alexis Lichine

A very dark brown British beer with a bitter taste. It is brewed from malt . . . dried at such high temperature that it has become brown or charred: . . . Similar to stout but not so strong, usually with a heavy creamy foam. The name is said to derive from the fact that it was the favourite drink of London porters.

     Encyclopedia of Wines and Spirits (1974)

WHISKY

**Winston
Churchill**
1874-1965

All this whisky business was quite a new departure in fashionable England. My father could never have drunk whisky except when shooting on a moor or in some dull chilly place. He lived in the age of 'brandy and soda'.

     Cited by Cyril Ray in *Spirits and Liqueurs* (1977)

**H. S.
Mackintosh**

Sublime beverage, supreme tipple,
The slick nectar (but the Haig's slicker!)
Which gods drew from divine nipple
And thick nights became a lot thicker . . .
He likes ladies and he loves liquor —
A large whisky and a small soda.

     'The Impossible Ballade of Whisky and Soda'

'Daisy Ashford'

Bernard always had a few prayers in the hall and some whiskey afterwards, as he was rather pious . . .

     The Young Visiters, [sic] (1919)

WHISKEY, IRISH *(UISGE BEATHA)*

J. K. Huysmans
1848-1907

[That] night Des Esseintes had no wish to listen to the taste of music; he confined himself to removing one note from the keyboard of his organ, carrying off a tiny cup which he had filled with genuine Irish whiskey. He settled down in his armchair ... and slowly sipped this fermented spirit of oats and barley, a pungent odour of creosote spreading through his mouth.

À Rebours (1882)

THE TOOLS AND THE TRADE

ADULTERATION

G. K. Chesterton
1874-1936

So that Lancashire merchants whenever they like
Can water the beer of a man in Klondike,
Or poison the beer of a man in Bombay . . .
  Songs of Education

Samuel Butler
1835-1902

The public buys . . . its milk, on the principle that
it is cheaper to do this than to keep a cow. So it is,
but the milk is more likely to be watered.
  *Notebooks, Material for a Proposed Sequel: Public
  Opinion*

H. D. Thoreau
1817-62

Some circumstantial evidence is very strong, as
when you find a trout in the milk.
  Journal

AROMAS

Lord Byron
1788-1824

The nursery still lisps out in all they utter —
Besides, they always smell of bread and butter.
> *Beppo*

And nearer as they came, a genial savour
Of certain stews, and roast meats, and pilaus,
Things which hungry mortals' eyes find favour.

Yet smelt roast meat, beheld a clear fire shine . . .
> *Don Juan*

Sadi of Persia
fl. 1200s

The smell of an onion from the mouth of the
lovely is sweeter than that of a rose in the hands
of the ugly.
> *Rose Garden: Hatefulness of Old Husbands*

Cicero
106-43 B.C.

Does it not betray itself by its odour?
> *Orator*

Anonymous

The stinking goat on yonder hill
Feeds all day long on chlorophyll.
> Cited by Katharine Whitehorn in *Cooking in a Bedsitter* (1963)

Alfred Sutro
1863-1933

. . . the plays of today . . . reek of sentiment till
you yearn for the smell of a cabbage.
> *The Man in the Stalls*

Francis Kilvert

The Vicar of St Ives says the smell of fish there is
sometimes so terrific as to stop the church clock.
> *Diary* (21 July 1870)

BARMAIDS AND BARMEN

John Masefield
1878-1967

And fifteen arms went round her waist,
(And then men ask, 'Are barmaids chaste?').
> 'The Everlasting Mercy'

J. Ainsworth Morgan

'Good morning, Mister, Sir or Count,
    What will it be today?'
And Frank awaits the deft reply:

'The same as yesterday'.
'To Frank Meier' (head barman at The Ritz, Paris, 1921-47)

Anonymous

... the fearful injury wrought upon young men ... by the seductive influence of young and exquisitely dressed barmaids in the saloons and back bars of several Adelaide hotels. These girls are generally of Melbourne or Sydney extraction ... their attraction heightened by artificial means, they dispensed liquors and toyed with the youthful gommeux.

Reader's letter to *Adelaide Advertiser* (1884)

Colin Thiele

... With breast and buttocks firm as trees
The barmaid-waitress blooms and sways,
And drinking timbermen appraise
How thighs grow upwards from the knees,
And tractor drivers' glances state
That doors they know of have no locks,
And love wears deftly zippered frocks.
When sudden spring and moonlight mate

And shearers ask for leg and tart:
No matter what the table lacks,
These come to them as midnight snacks
Kept hot and served with lusty art.

'Up-country Pubs' (1970)

BARS

Dorothy Parker
1893-1967

Some men, some men
Cannot pass a
Bar-room.
(Wait about, and hang about, and that's the way it
goes.)

'Chant for Dark Hours'

John Collier

This bar, near Leicester Square ... could satisfy at one and the same time the appetite, thirst and imagination, for to the mediocre sandwiches and drinks providence had added half a dozen ladies ... one could recognize immediately [as] the mature English prostitute.

Cited by X. M. Boulestin in *Ease and Endurance* (1948)

BATTER

'Bon Viveur'
[John and Fanny
Cradock]

If you wish to fry fish in batter, for pity's sake never let the batter be like those terrible old winding sheets of oily flab beloved by British fish and chip shops!

Daily Telegraph Cook's Book (1964)

BOCUSE, PAUL

Robert Courtine

... a curious food man ... With a chef's hat full of wit, a sparkling eye, a light hand to lift his glass, he is a swashbuckler of the drip pans, a juggler of pots, and a poet of stews ... He is a host of eternity, a kind of Medici of food. He pushes a button, and presto ...

Feasts of a Militant Gastronome, (1973)

BRILLAT-SAVARIN

An admirer

He left the world like a satisfied diner leaving the banquet room.

Cited by M. F. K. Fisher in her translation of *Physiologie du Goût* (1971)

M. F. K. Fisher
(trans.)

He was thickset, with more than a hint of paunch ... but with handsome legs, he admitted blandly of himself. He could be a tender and sensitive lover ... He was an amiable dinner companion, and at times a witty one ... He liked to eat with pretty women, sing to them, tease them. Above all he liked to look at them, no matter whether his eye was purely voluptuous or was tempered by a physician's appraisal or a confessor's pity.

Physiology of Taste

Marquis de
Cussy

Brillat-Savarin ate copiously and ill; he chose little, talked dully, had no vivacity in his looks, and was absorbed at the end of a repast.

L'Art Culinaire

Emile de Labédollière

Physically he was very tall, so that he had been named the drum-major of the Court of Appeals. Since he enjoyed lengthy meals, all the while managing to avoid indigestion and tipsiness, he had acquired a girth proportionate to his weight. His fleshy face was none too expressive. His careless way of dressing, with a generous shirt collar and full trousers bagging over his shoes, gave him the appearance of an undistinguished bumpkin. Usually he preferred to listen rather than talk; he hardly seemed to come to life until the end of a good dinner, and then his conversation had the subtle effervescence of champagne which at last had been poured from its long imprisonment; but people with whom he had no close relationship state almost unanimously that he was uncommunicative, heavy, and absent-minded, and that he never unveiled in his meetings with them the classicism, the finesse, and the wide general knowledge which he proved in *Physiologie du Goût* to possess.

Introduction to the 1852 edition of *Physiologie du Goût*

BUTCHERS

Samuel Johnson
1709-84

When a butcher tells you his heart bleeds for his country, he has, in fact, no uneasy feeling.
Boswell's *Life of Johnson*

John Gay
1688-1732

Butchers! Whose hands are dy'd with blood's foul
  stain
And always foremost in the hangman's train.
  Trivia

Thomas B. Aldrich
1836-1907

Bonnet in hand, obsequious and discreet,
The butcher that served Shakespeare with his
  meat
Doubtless esteemed him little, as a man,
We know not how the market prices ran.
  Points of View

CHAFING DISH

C. Herman Senn
Oh, I am a festive chafing dish,
I foam, and froth, and bubble,
I sing the song of meat and fish,
And save a deal of trouble.

In kitchen realm and dining hall
The housewife now is able,
When I respond unto her call,
To cook dinner on the table.

Chafing Dish and Casserole Cookery (1908)

COOKS AND CHEFS

Ben Jonson
1572-1637
A master cook! why he's the man of men
For a professor; he designs, he draws,
He paints, he carves, he builds, he fortifies,
Makes citadels of curious fowl and fish.
Some he dry-ditches, some moats around with
broths,
Mounts marrow bones, cuts fifty-angled custards,
Rears bulwark pies; and for his outer works,
He raiseth ramparts of immortal crust,
And teacheth all the tactics at one dinner —
What ranks, what files to put his dishes in,
The whole art military! Then he knows
The influence of the stars upon his meats,
And all their seasons, tempers and qualities;
And so to fit his relishes and sauces,
He has nature in a pot, 'bove all the chemists
Or airy brethren of the rosy cross.
He is an architect, an engineer,
A soldier, a physician, a philosopher,
A general mathematician.

Cited in The Gentle Art of Cookery

Paul Gauguin
1848-1903
Many excellent cooks are spoilt by going into the
arts.

In Cournos' Modern Plutarch

Martial
43-104
I seem to you cruel and gluttonous when I beat
my cook for sending up a bad dinner. If that appears too trifling a cause, say for what cause you
would have a cook flogged?

Epigrams

Menander
342-291

Nobody ever escaped punishment for unrighteous treatment of a cook.

Dyskolos

Richard Beckett

What hope has the poor sod of a chef got in a world where most people prefer the taste of MSG-encrusted packet soups . . . to real chicken-noodle soup . . . It's the pissing-in-the-wind syndrome alive and well and abroad again. Australians, by and large, get the bloody food they deserve.

Nation Review (1974)

**Balthazar
Gerbier**
1591?-1667

Too many cooks spoil the broth.

Discourse of Building (1662)

Owen Meredith
1831-91

We may live without poetry, music and art;
We may live without conscience and live without heart;
We may live without friends, we may live without books,
But civilised man cannot live without cooks.

Lucile

Thomas Fuller
1654-1734

A good cook is known by his knife.

Gnomologia

**J. A. McNeill
Whistler**
1834-1903

I don't see why people make such a to-do about choosing a new cook. There is only one thing that is absolutely essential. I always ask at once, 'Do you drink?', and if she says 'No!', I bow politely and say that I am very sorry but I fear she will not suit. All *good* cooks drink.

Attributed in *Life was Worth Living*

**'Saki' [H. H.
Munro]**
1870-1916

The cook was a good cook, as cooks go;
And as cooks go, she went.

Reginald on Besetting Sins

E. M. Delafield

Memo: Must speak to cook about sending in a minute segment of sponge cake, remains of one which, to my certain recollection, made its first appearance more than ten days ago. Also, why perpetual and unappetising procession of small rock cakes?

Diary of a Provincial Lady

Raphael Holinshed

In the number of dishes and changes of meat, the nobility of England (whose cooks for the most part are musical-headed Frenchmen and strangers) do most exceed, sith there is not a day in manner passeth over their heads wherein they have not only beef, mutton, veal and lamb, kid, pork, coney, capon, pig or so many of these that the season yieldeth, but also some portion of the red and fallow deer, besides a great variety of fish and wild fowl, and thereto sundry other delicacies.

Chronicle of England (1577)

Robert Courtine

There is a well known joke in France about Madame de Brinvilliers, the famous poisoner, to whom some gastronome compared a bad chef, saying, 'The only difference between La Brinvilliers and him is that *he* had good intentions!'

Feasts of a Militant Gastronome (1973)

CUISINE

Curnonsky
1872-¿

'Cuisine' means that
Things taste just like what they are!
  'To Melanie Rouat'

Robert Courtine

But there have also been countless disappointments provoked by French cuisine! The cuisine of chefs who are like the frogs of the La Fontaine fable, each of whom dreams of being fat as a bull, but ends up full of air because a Parisian celebrity, a lady of culinary charity, or some hustling advertising executive has assured them they have genius.

Feasts of a Militant Gastronome (1973)

Quentin Crewe

. . . a cuisine — a word which suggests a certain confinement and rigidity, both of place and conduct.

Quentin Crewe's International Pocket Food Book (1980)

CUISINE MINCEUR

Michel Guérard

The mysterious and lovely Christine, who had doubtless already made up her mind to marry me some months later, whispered in my ear, very softly and nicely, 'You know, it would be a good thing for you if you could lose a few kilos'.

What a jolt — I had to swallow my pride and lose some of my corporation to win Christine's heart ... I wanted to produce a complete festival of light meals for slimming, with salads as fresh as children's laughter, gleaming fish, the heavy scent of forbidden peaches, and roast chickens as deliciously perfumed as those of my childhood picnics.

Cuisine Minceur, trans. by Caroline Conran (1977)

CUISINE DU SOLEIL

Roger Verge

My father was a blacksmith ... the tender bouquets of vegetables he brought were so full of flavour and aroma that all that was needed was the addition of a few of the big rosy strips of pork fat which sizzled in the big cast-iron pot.

This was the 'cuisine heureuse', which consisted of marrying natural products with one another, of finding simple harmonies and enhancing the flavour of each ingredient by contact with another complementary flavour ... It is the antithesis of cooking to impress.

Cuisine of the Sun, trans. by Caroline Conran (1979)

CUTLERY

T. S. Eliot
1888-1965

I have measured out my life with coffee spoons.
Love Song of J. Alfred Prufrock

Anonymous

... the German Blade Museum [at Solingen] ... with nearly 3000 objects ... ranging from a four-pronged wooden fork for cannibalistic feasts on Fiji to plastic stirrers for airline passengers; from a

flint knife dated 300,000 B.C. to graceful art nou-
veau flatware, with sinuous plant motifs twining
about the silver handles.

'The German Blade Museum', *Lufthansa's Germany*

C. S. Calverley
1831-84
Dashed the bold fork through pies of pork;
O'er hard-boiled eggs the salt-spoon shook.

'The Palace'

Gertrude Harris
It is well known that a chef's knife, like a cow-
boy's pony, will not permit a stranger to ride it.

Pots and Pans (1975)

ESCOFFIER

Stephen Watts
'Never complicate' was one of Escoffier's maxims.
[He also] believed that food being served really
hot added twenty-five per cent to its virtue . . .
The Ritz does not . . . put any stress on the fact
that Pêche Melba originated in its kitchens.

The Ritz (1963)

Elizabeth David
I do not invariably feel confidence in Escoffier — I
find, for example, that his fruit and ice-cream
dishes are unnecessarily recherché and fussy, although . . . the overworking of food and a profes-
sional reluctance to present a peach . . . as nature
made it was the tendency in [his] time.

Spices, Salt and Aromatics in the English Kitchen (1970)

ETERNAL QUEST FOR NOVELTY

David Dale
French entrepreneur Alain Chatillon is about to
launch snails' eggs as a new delicacy. He expects
to sell them in England for around £500 ($A1061)
a kilo [2.2 lb.]. [He] first tried snails' eggs in Tibet
. . . found them to have a 'complex subtle flavour
rapidly followed by a bitter aftertaste' . . . He 're-
fines' the eggs . . . in the Pyrenees by steeping
them in brine for 30 to 40 days, then flavouring
them with herbs, almond extract and a dash of
pepper. He exports them to Belgium, Switzerland,

Canada and the United States. Fortnum and Mason was testing the eggs [as] 'We do have some rather adventurous customers ... we often get asked for unusual things'.

'Stay in Touch', *Sydney Morning Herald* (1986)

FLAVOUR

Martial
43-104

Whether woodcock or partridge, what does it matter, if the flavour be the same? A partridge is dearer, and thus has better flavour.

Epigrams

Lord Byron
1788-1824

... like vinegar from wine —
A sad, sour, sober beverage — by time
Is sharpen'd from its high celestial flavour
Down to a very homely household savour.

Don Juan

Ian Bersten
[Belaroma
Coffee M/D]

There seems to be an increasing trend for people to produce food with less flavour — a case of the bland leading the bland.

Comment in a talk on 'Cocoa' on ABC radio (1986)

GASTRONOMY

Brillat-Savarin
1755-1826

... the intelligent knowledge of whatever concerns man's nourishment.

Physiologie du Goût

GROCERS

G. K. Chesterton
1874-1936

God made the wicked grocer
For a mystery and a sign,
That men might shun the awful shop
And go to inns to dine.

'Song Against Grocers'

Mrs C. F. Leyel

Grocers were descended from the pepperers ... and spicers ... who amalgamated in 1345 and ... adopted the more comprehensive title of engrosser, from the Latin *grossarius*. In a grocer's shop at that time was to be found every sort of medicine, root and herb, gums, spices, oils and ointments. Syrups and waters, turpentine and plaisters ranged side by side with dried fruit and confectionery, pepper and ginger.

The Magic of Herbs (1926)

HOSPITALITY

John Lyly
c.1554-1606

Fish and guests in three days are stale.
Euphues (1580)

Ambrose Bierce
1842-c.1914

Hospitality: the virtue which induces us to feed and lodge certain persons who are not in need of food and lodging.
The Enlarged Devil's Dictionary

Samuel Pepys
1633-1703

Good and much company, and a good dinner . . .
Diary (1663)

T. B. Aldrich
1836-1907

If my best wines mislike thy taste
And my best service win thy frown
Then tarry not, I bid thee haste;
There's many another inn in town.
Quits

**E. R. L.
Laboulaye**
1811-83

The first day a man is a guest,
The second a burden, the third a pest.
Abdallah

HOTELIERS

Charles Ritz

I know about details, and if I have introduced or perfected a hundred details in my time, I shall be content. After all, no chef has even invented a hundred dishes.
Cited in Stephen Watts' *The Ritz* (1963)

HOTELS

Thomas Wood
Meals at small hotels in Western Australia are usually square. Tea always is; and one menu card could be used throughout the State. It would say 'Soup, fried steak with two veg., corned beef or cold mutton, sweets'.

Cobbers (1931)

Ogden Nash
1902-71
I know a renegade hotel,
I also know I hate it well,
An inn so vile, an inn so shameless,
For very disgust I leave it nameless . . .

'Traveller's Rest', *The Face is Familiar* (1942)

Artemus Ward
1834-67
I prefer temperance hotels — although they sell worse liquor than any other kind of hotels.

Temperance

Carol Willson and John Goode
Perhaps you can't judge a book by its cover, but a recent bout of hotel life convinced us that you can assess a hotel by its bathrooms . . . In this age of automation, hotel bathrooms could only be designed by robots.

'You Can Judge a Hotel By Its Loos', *Sydney Morning Herald* (1984)

INNKEEPERS AND INNS

Samuel Johnson
1709-84
No sir, there is nothing which has yet been contrived by man, by which so much happiness is produced, as by a good tavern or inn.

Boswell's *Life of Johnson*

Foster Fyans
fl. 1850s
Of all the impositions inflicted on mankind, an inn in the district is the most dreadful abomination. It appears to me the licensee considers only one duty . . . that is, to persecute and victimise the traveller . . . his sole object is money.

Letter from Commissioner of Crown Lands, Portland District of Victoria, to Charles La Trobe, Governor of the colony

Prince Pükler-
Muskau
fl. 1820s

As I entered the inn [in Cheltenham], which I might almost call magnificent, and ascended the snow-white stair-case ornamented with a gilt-bronze railing and trod in fresh and brilliant carpets, lighted by two servants to my room, I gave myself up, *con amore*, to the feeling of comfort which can be found in perfection nowhere but England ... all that a man can promote with money.

    Cited by Philippa Pullar in *Consuming Passions*

Plato
c. 428-347 B.C.

Helots who receive us as friends and treat us like captives, extorting huge and abominable ransoms.

    Cited in *Antipasto*

Ellen Clacy

... a neat inn after the English style ... The bedrooms are so arranged as to separate nobs from snobs ...

    A Lady's Visit to the Gold Diggings of Australia (1853)

G. K. Chesterton
1874-1936

The righteous minds of innkeepers
Induce them now and then
To crack a bottle with a friend
Or treat unmoneyed men,
But who hath seen the Grocer
Treat housemaids to his teas
Or crack a bottle of fish-sauce
Or stand a man a cheese?

    'The Song Against Grocers'

KITCHEN UTENSILS

Thomas Brown

... What a void in the world would their art leave
    behind!
Their chronometer spits — their intense sala-
    manders —
Their ovens — their pots, that can soften old
    ganders,
All vanish'd for ever — their miracles o'er,
And the *Marmite Perpetuelle* bubbling no more!

    The Fudge Family in Paris (1818)

KITCHENS

Sir Walter Scott
1771-1832

. . . in dark nook aloof,
. . . of sea-fowl dried, and solands store,
And gammons of the tusky boar
And savoury haunch of deer.

A Scottish kitchen, as described in *Marmion*

LA NOUVELLE CUISINE

Anonymous

La nouvelle cuisine was christened in October 1973 by Henri Gault and Christian Millau, in an article in the Gault-Millau magazine called 'Vive la Nouvelle Cuisine Francaise' . . . The chefs — Roger Verge, Michel Guerard, Paul Bocuse, the two Troisgros brothers, Charles Barrier and eight others — had all been influenced by Fernand Point (died 1955) at La Pyramide in Vienne, or by Alexandre Dumaine at the Côte d'Or at Saulieu . . .

'The Novel Nouvelle', *SMH Good Living* (1985)

Jean and Pierre Troisgros

Our father, Jean-Baptiste Troisgros, always said that cooking should be a carefully balanced reflection of all the good things of the earth . . . he did love good ingredients . . . and so do we. We get our snails from the schoolboys of Roanne . . . we only buy produce that is in season and of irreproachable high quality and absolute freshness . . . As it becomes simpler and lighter the chef's art is getting nearer to the home cook's art . . .

The Nouvelle Cuisine of Jean and Pierre Troisgros trans. Caroline Conran (1980)

Note: one recipe reads –
  for the farce
  450g [1 lb] mild ham
  1½ egg whites . . .
How it is possible to dissect an egg white has never been explained! *J. G.*

Robert Courtine

The turnips [prepared by the Troisgros brothers at Le Club 33, Brussels] merely braised, would have been enough escort for the duck liver with its gamey overtones. The Perigueux sauce that covered them was no more than a stylistic performance ... distracting from the Racinian purity that should characterise a dish of that type ... if this meal had not been prepared by the Troisgros, one would have started out with Georges Sand and ended up with nothingness — that is to say, Francois Sagan!

Feasts of a Militant Gastronome (1973)

Barbara Abell

You're facing a rebellion
(From your customers, I mean),
We've left the pie and sauce brigade
But DETEST Nouvelle Cuisine.

We do not seek the laden plate
That makes us groan, but — Jeeze,
We look for more than breast of quail
Served up with three snow peas.

At evening's end we find that we
Have spent a tidy sum,
Yet don't know which is emptier,
Our wallet or our tum.

So heed this timely warning
And restore the Horn of Plenty,
Or you'll find that we will head, *en masse*,
Back to the Four'n Twenty*.

'To (most) restaurateurs', *Age, Melbourne Living* (1985)
*A well-known manufacturer of pies (q.v) in Australia

MACROBIOTICS

Craig and Ann Sams

In the early 1960s, many ... were attracted to the ideas of Georges Ohsawa, a Japanese who had rediscovered the importance of dietary balance in traditional Eastern medicine ... [He] taught macrobiotics, a dietary system in which brown rice plays a major role.

The Brown Rice Cookbook (1980)

MARINADE

Katharine Whitehorn 'Marinade — the Poor Man's Fridge'.
Cooking in a Bedsitter (1963)

Dorris McFerran Townsend Long ago . . . home cooks learned to soak meat in wine to give their family's teeth a fighting chance . . . Marinades generally have three kinds of ingredients: an acid — wine, vinegar or lemon juice — to attack and tenderise tough fibres; fat — oil, or less usually, melted butter — to make the meat juicy; and seasonings . . . to enhance the meat's flavour with their own.
The Cook's Companion (1978)

MENU

Andre Launay . . . the Duke of Brunswick who, as late as 1541, was the first to draw up a list of all the foods his chef could prepare, so that his guests could reserve their appetites for their favourite dishes.
Caviare and After (1964)

Prosper Montagné . . . a 'bill of fare', which in old French was called an *escriteau* . . . [A] list of dishes served '. . . for the nuptial supper of Master Baulde Cuvillon' in 1571 . . . preserved in the archives of the Northern Department of France.
Larousse Gastronomique (1961)

NOVELTY

G. A. Escoffier *Novelty!* It is the prevailing cry; it is imperiously demanded by everyone . . . What feats of ingenuity have we not been forced to perform . . . to meet our customers' wishes? . . . I have ceased counting the nights spent in the attempt to discover new combinations, when, completely broken with fatigue of a heavy day, my body ought to have been at rest.
A Guide to Modern Cookery (1907)

Charles Chantraine
... the creation of original dishes is a demanding art ... To build a culinary art of one's own requires experience, patience, and care.

La Cuisine Chantraine (1967)

PANTRY

Wilma Pezzini
From the elegant *villa signorile* to the simple *rustico di campagna* ... there is hardly a Tuscan home without a pantry.

The Tuscan Cookbook (1978)

PRESSURE COOKER

John Evelyn
1620-1706
I went this Afternoon to a Supper ... which was all dressed [cooked] in Monsieur Papins Digestorie; by which the hardest bones of Biefe itselfe & Mutton, were, without water or other liquor ... made as soft as cheese, produc'd an incredible quantity of Gravie, & for close, a Gelie, made of bones of biefe ... nothing exceeded the Pigeons, which tasted just as if baked in a *pie*, all these being stewed in their own juice.

Diary (1682)

Note: Could this be the first description of a pressure cooker? J. G.

Carol Willson and John Goode
... using a pressure cooker regularly can be like living on the brink. Indeed, the shock of mishap, while of little personal danger, can be as shattering as the eruption of Mt St Helens, or even Lamington in Papua New Guinea ... [loss] of the plug releases a centimetre-diameter fountain of minestrone ... or some similarly pungent and deeply-coloured aromatic brew, that spurts forth with all the energy of Old Faithful ...

'Yes, we really like dancing on a volcano*', 'Good Living' *Sydney Morning Herald* (1982)

* Comte de Salvandy, 'We're dancing on a volcano'

PUBS AND TAVERNS

Edward FitzGerald
1809-83

I heard a voice within the Tavern cry
'Awake, my little ones, and fill the Cup,
Before Life's Liquor in its Cup be dry' . . .
I often wonder what the Vintners buy
One half so precious as the Goods they sell.

Rubai'yat of Omar Khayyam

Oliver Goldsmith
1728-74

Low lies that house where nut-brown draughts
    inspired,
Where greybeard mirth and smiling toil retired;
Where village statesmen talked with looks
    profound,
And news much older than their ale, went round.

The Deserted Village

Gareth Powell

All Australian pubs look as if they have been designed by an architect with a fixation on railway
urinals . . . a decent pub offers you snacks at the
bar . . . morsels to encourage the thirst, delight the
palate and bring a note of civilisation to the pro-
ceedings. A packet of potato crisps, sold at an
exorbitant profit and tasting like cuttings from last
year's *Herald*, lightly fried, is no substitute.

'There Are No Good Pubs In Australia', *Sydney
Morning Herald* (1985)

Horatio Smith
1779-1849

Champagne doth not a Luncheon make
Nor caviar a meal;
Men gluttonous and rich may take
These till they've made them ill.
If I've potatoes to my chop,
And after that have cheese,
Angels in Pond and Spiers's shop
Serve no such luxuries.

'At the Cock Tavern'

RECIPES

Roger Verge

A recipe is not meant to be followed exactly — it
is a canvas on which you can embroider. Impro-

vise and invent. Add the zest of this, a drop or
two of that, a tiny pinch of the other . . .

Cuisine of the Sun, trans. Caroline Conran (1979)

RESTAURANTS

Antonia Williams
M. Ritz introduced impeccable service, cooking and decorations at the Savoy; he made it a place where men took their wives, not their mistresses.

'Spotlight on the Dinner Party', *Vogue* (1979)

Ogden Nash
1902-71
I know a little restaurant
Behind a brownstone stoop
Where *pottage du jour* is French
For a can of onion soup.

Try it Suns. and Hols.: It's Closed Then

E. V. Lucas
1868-1938
The art of life is to be so well known at a good restaurant that you can pay with a cheque.

Over Bemerton's

Philippa Pullar   In the eighteenth century, one could only eat at
special cookshops or inns. But in 1765 . . . Boulan-
ger, a soup-seller, called his soups by the special
name of *restaurant* — restorative. Their sale was so
successful he wanted to enlarge his menu, but
since he was not a member of the *traiteurs* corporation — eating-house keepers — he was not
permitted to serve ragouts. Instead he offered his
customers sheeps' feet in white sauce . . . not a
ragout. Boulanger's sheeps' feet in white sauce
became famous all over Paris. From 1786 onwards
the great cuisiniers opened restaurants, nearly all
of which were famous for a particular speciality.

Consuming Passions (1970)

Oscar Wilde   She tried to found a salon, but only succeeded in
1854-1900   opening a restaurant.

Picture of Dorian Gray

X. M. Boulestin   We dined at a restaurant in Lisle Street [Soho, in
London] . . . The bread there was French, the pro-
prietor Swiss, the waiters Belgian, the chef Italian,
the cooking quite beyond analysis, and the menu
composed of a strange language: *risetto à anglaise
rosbif à la inglese* . . . As for the wine, the establish-
ment not being licensed, a waiter had to go and
fetch it — pure Australian Burgundy — and the
coffee, trying to be Turkish, resembled a muddy
chicory infusion.

Ease and Endurance (1948)

WARTIME BRITAIN

Frances   A swelling stream of citizens . . . following . . .
Partridge   notices marked 'British Restaurant' [to eat] an
enormous all-beige meal; starting with beige
soup, thickened to a consistency of paste, followed by beige mince, full of lumps and gar-
nished with beige beans and a few beige potatoes,
thin beige apple stew and a sort of skilly . . . all
beige also.

'Gastronomy in Beige', *A Pacifist's War* (1978)

RESTAURATEURS

Walter James La Mere Fillioux at 73, Rue Duquesne, Lyons, served very few dishes and served them to perfection ... for thirty years offered every day virtually the same luncheon, virtually the same dinner ... the principal dish every evening was chicken with sliced truffles slipped under the skin and poached in a bouillon; artichoke bottoms and *foie gras* invariably followed.

Some of Lyons' leading citizens arranged a dinner at her restaurant in honour of a celebrated visiting actress. As a mark of special grace, lobsters had been added to the standard bill of fare. Just after they sat down, the unspeakable thing was spoken. The actress asked Madame if the lobsters were fresh! La Fillioux turned pale, turned red, turned voluble and turned the dinner party on to the pavement.

Antipasto (1957)

Peter Smark Stephanie Alexander is the Second Lady of Melbourne cuisine ... and has prospered and moved to much posher premises through an insistence on telling the market what it should want, and seeing the customers accept her dicta ... Hermann Schneider of Two Faces is renowned for attention to detail ... There is a suggestion ... that it is the diner's obligation to please the management ...

'From Melbourne, 0/28 Gives Us the TV Dinner', *SMH TV Guide* (1984)

ROASTING

Arthur Machen Roasting is almost obsolete; and at one of the most famous 'Old English' resorts in London, where they do roast, they hang beef, veal and lamb on one spit and baste all three joints in the common gravy ...

Preface to 1926 edition of *Physiologie du Goût*

Anonymous *To Roast Meats, etc.* The first thing ... is to have a strong steady fire, or a clear brisk one, according to the size and weight of the joint that is put down to the spit. A cook who does not attend to this will prove herself totally incompetent ... All roasting should be done in the open air, to ventilate the meat from its gross fumes, otherwise it become baked instead of roasted. The joint should be ... at such a distance from the fires as to imbibe the heat rather quickly, otherwise its plumpness and good quality will be gradually dried up, and it will turn shrivelly, and look meagre ... When it is warm, begin to baste it well, which prevents the nutritive juices escaping; and, if required, additional dripping must be used ...

English 18th Century Cookery

SARTOR RESARTUS

Cole Lesley

The weather in August became grillingly hot with high humidity and so, although the kitchen was large and pleasant, one wore as little as possible while the oven and gas-rings were on. Noel, alone one morning, was in fact wearing nothing at all except Doris's little plastic apron patterned with rosebuds, when a dignified gentleman appeared and explained ... that he was the Bishop of Bermuda ... Would the Bishop give him *one* moment to see how his vol-au-vent cases were getting on? Bending over to see ... involved exposing his bare bottom ... and by the time he straightened himself ... the Bishop had fled, and never called again.

The Life of Noel Coward (1978)

SHOPPING

Charpentier

In France the market basket is an object of the utmost significance. If it is true that England's battles have been won on her cricket fields, then it is not to be questioned that the greatness of France has been nourished from her market baskets.

Those Rich and Great Ones (1935)

SIMPSON'S RESTAURANT, LONDON

Anonymous

Simpson's for example! In we rush from the roar of the Strand. A long, dark, sweltering room is before us; no bright-eyed *dame du comptoi*; no shining, flashing mirrors; no waiters to glide at your nod; hot, roaring guests, shouting waiters, men in cotton coats shoving about large dishes of steaming meat on rolling tables, and you eat your dinner in an atmosphere full of gin, fat, steam, and gabble ... and where you are choked by foul air ...

The Irish Quarterly Review (1858)

J. P. de Oliveira-Martins

... in the classic tavern of Simpson's, the real one in the Strand ... They gave me a slice of meat swimming in fat, a piece fit for Pantagruel, cut out on the spot from a sanguinary heap carried about among the tables.

Cited by Pullar in *Consuming Passions* (1970)

TEACHING COOKING

Shizuo Tsuji

The way of teaching every Japanese art has traditionally been an imperfect passing-down from master to disciple of jealously-guarded personal interpretations. The master never explained; he merely demonstrated. And it was left to the more perceptive students to glean what they could of the master's art — filling in the gaps with their own ingenuity.

Japanese Cooking — A Simple Art (1980)

TERMINOLOGY

W. St Leger
fl. 1890

There is a fine stuffed chavender,
A chavender, or chubb,
That decks the rural pavender,
The pavender or pub,
Wherein I eat my gravender,
My gravender or grub.

A False Gallop of Analogies

WAITERS AND WAITRESSES

Anonymous   A Waiter's Manual suggests that any of the following replies are appropriate when a customer
complains 'There's a fly in my soup':
1. Ssh! Everybody will want one!
2. What do you expect for a dime —
   elephants?
3. Wait until you see the coffee!
4. That's all right. How much can a fly drink?
5. Force of habit, Sir. Our chef used to be a
   tailor.

Cited by Bennett Cerf in *Laughing Stock* (1945)

Anonymous   'Waiter,' commanded a big shot in a little restaurant, 'bring us two orders of guiseppe ver-
ticelli.' 'Your pardon,' said the waiter gently, 'but
that's the proprietor.'

Ibid.

WRITERS ON FOOD

Christopher   [Raymond] Postgate was an eighteenth-century
Driver   man ... fiercely English in his tastes and affec-
tions. He would not seriously have expected to
encounter roast cygnet very often ... but would
have been puzzled by an England that lost its taste
for herring ... he had a demotic touch and experience that were denied ... to André Simon, the
French historian of the English wine trade [who]
had become the symbol of gourmandise in his
adopted country ... [His] output of books and
articles was prolific to the point of blatant pot-
boiling. A peasant at heart, as he was the first to
acknowledge, Simon was treated by his monied
... circle of British — and American — wine-
lovers with deferential respect ...

Mrs [Elizabeth] David's background could hardly have been more English: descended directly
from a Victorian Home Secretary and a Conservative MP ... educated at an ill-fed English girls'
school, married for a while to a British diplomat.

She tried both painting and acting before turning in her late thirties to cooking and writing . . . the literary curiosity and obsessional accuracy of a born writer and researcher brought her books to life and made them work.

The British at Table 1940-1980 (1983)

BREAD, CHEESE AND OTHER BASICS

BIRDS' NEST

Andre Launay

If it wasn't for the fact that Chinese cookery, together with French cookery, is generally recognised by top gourmets as being the best in the world, one might hesitate to include birds' nest soup . . . knowing it to be made only with a consommé base and bird spit. But epicures consider it a luxury . . .

Caviare and After (1964)

BOUILLABAISSE

¿Méry

For fasting on Fridays, one day, an abbess
From a convent in Marseilles invented bouillabaisse.
And never since then have people been ungrateful . . .

'Bouillabaisse', in Charles Monselet's *La Cuisiniere Poetique*

Marcel Pagner

. . . bouillabaisse originated as a fishermen's dish. [What remained unsold of the] day's catch was thrown into a cauldron . . . and once the soup had boiled (*bouilli*) they would ladle it down (*abaisser*) to their plates . . . Whence *bouille-abaisse*.

Cited in *Feasts of a Militant Gastronome* (1973)

H. L. Mencken
1880-1956

All the great villanies from history, from the murder of Abel onward, have been perpetrated by sober men, and chiefly by teetotallers. But all of the charming and beautiful things from the Song of Songs to *bouillabaisse*, and from the nine Beethoven symphonies to the Martini cocktail, have been given to humanity by men who, when the

hour came, turned from tap water to something
with colour in it . . .

Selected Prejudices

BREAD

Epicurus
c.342-270 B.C.

Plain fare gives as much pleasure as a costly diet,
while bread and water confer the highest possible
pleasure when they are brought to hungry lips.

Letter to Menoeceus

Francis Bacon
1561-1626

Acorns were good until bread was found.

Colours of Good and Evil

Chaucer
1340?-1400

And let us honest wives eat barley bread.

Prologue to the Wife of Bath's Tale, trans. Pope

Mark Twain
1835-1910

. . . European bread — fair enough, good enough,
after a fashion, but cold . . . and tough, and un-
sympathetic; and never any change . . . any
variety — always the same tiresome thing.

'European Diet', *A Tramp Abroad*

**Laurens van der
Post**

Ethiopians grow . . . teff, the finest, subtlest and
most delicate member of the millet family. It is
made into a batter which is allowed to ferment
. . . and is then poured on to a flat iron skillet to
cook. The result is called *injera* . . . I can never
understand the disparaging remarks European
travellers . . . make about injera. John Gunther . . .
describes injera as 'looking like an old inner tube'
. . . Dervla Murphy . . . says it tastes 'like foam
rubber'. This is just not true. It is a subtle and
indispensable supplement to the enjoyment of a
meal.

First Catch Your Eland (1977)

Charpentier

At Christmas time, her bread would acquire a
smoother texture, was softer to the touch and had
an exciting flavour. How was it done? Two
spoons of olive oil, two of sugar and four of butter
worked into the bread dough . . .

Those Rich and Great Ones (1935)

Thomas Hood 1799-1845	Who hath not met with home-made bread, A heavy compound of putty and lead. *Miss Kilmansegg*
Dylan Thomas 1914-53	This bread was once the oat . . . Man in the day or wind at night Laid the crops low . . . 'This Bread I Bake'
Compton Mackenzie 1883-1972	You are offered a piece of bread and butter that feels like a damp handkerchief and sometimes, when cucumber is added to it, like a wet one. *Vestal Fire* (1923)
Lila Perl	As bread of precious wheat flour was not to be wasted [in New Orleans] even when it became stale, the thrifty French wives soaked it in a sweetened mixture of milk and eggs, fried it in butter, and served it with honey or preserves. They call this dish *pain perdu* ('lost bread') but it has come to be known all over the United States as French toast. *Hunter's Stew and Hangtown Fry* (1977)
W. M. Thackeray 1811-63	Would you know how he first met her? She was cutting bread and butter. 'The Sorrows of Werther'
Jonathan Swift 1667-1745	Bachelor's fare; bread and cheese, and kisses. *Polite Conversation*

BREAKFAST CEREALS

Fred Allen	He dreamed he was eating Shredded Wheat and woke up to find the mattress half gone. *Comedy program in USA*
Anonymous	On Nevski Bridge a Russian stood Chewing his beard for lack of food. Said he, 'It's tough this stuff to eat But a darn sight better than shredded wheat!' 'The Iron Curtain', cited in Silcock, *Verse and Worse* (1952)

E. V. Lucas
1868-1938

Oatmeal marks not only the child's breakfast, it is thus the favourite food of the Edinburgh reviewers. Thus do extremes meet.

Domesticities

BRIE

Oswald Burdett

Brie invites hospitality ... [it] must be creamy, oozing, *coulant* throughout. Its colour is nearer butter than that of cream ... the rind of Brie is less feltlike than Camembert's, softer, thinner ... more an extension of the cheese than a different substance surrounding it ... For Brie to be surpassable seems impossible.

A Little Book of Cheese (1935)

Richard Hovey
1864-1900

A jug and a mug at every place,
And a biscuit or two with Brie!
Three stone jugs of Cruiskeen Lawn,
And a cheese like crusted foam!

The Kavanagh

BUTTER

A. A. Milne
1882-1956

The King asked
The Queen, and
The Queen asked
The Dairymaid:
'Could we have some butter for
The Royal slice of bread?'

'The King's Breakfast', *When We Were Very Young*

**Hermann
Goering**
1893-1946

Guns will make us powerful; butter only makes us fat.

Broadcast, 1936

Charles Lamb
1775-1834

A tub of butter, contemplated by him, amounts to a Platonic idea. He understands a leg of mutton in its quiddity. He stands wondering about the commonplace materials of life, like primeval man with the sun and stars about him.

Essay on the actor, Munden

Mark Twain
1835-1910

[European] butter — the sham and tasteless . . . no salt in it, and made of goodness knows what.

'European Diet', *A Tramp Abroad*

CAMEMBERT

Oswald Burdett

Camembert originated in 1791 in the commune of that name [Madame Harel, its inventor] . . . a genuine ripe Camembert . . . shows the heights of delicacy to which soft cheeses can aspire. Even the most mild palate cannot be offended by it . . . a hard Camembert can be nursed at home if it is wrapped in a damp cloth and kept in a moderately warm temperature, until the whole shall have reached a semi-oozy creaminess.

A Little Book of Cheese (1935)

Camembert, like a ripe pear, needs to be eaten, as it were, upon the wing. It waits for no man beyond its prime . . . When over-ripe, it is unsightly to the eye, distasteful to the nose, unwholesome to the stomach.

Op. cit.

Evan Jones

No one is born with the knack of invariably picking a perfect example of a cheese with a thin skin and a creamy centre. It takes practice. 'Poking the rind, testing the elasticity of the cheese, predicting what it will be like, is a bit like dowsing . . .' Colette once said.

The Book of Cheese (1980)

CHEESE

R. L. Stevenson
1850-94

Many's the long night I've dreamed of cheese — toasted mostly.

Treasure Island

W. H. Auden
1907-73

A poet's hope: to be,
like some valley cheese,
local, but prized elsewhere.

'Shorts II', *Collected Poems 1958-71*

| **Charles de Gaulle** 1890-1970 | The French will only be united under threat of danger. Nobody can simply bring together a country that has 265 kinds of cheese. |
| | Speech during elections of 1951 |

| **Charles Lamb** 1775-1834 | Your cheese is the best I ever tasted. Mary . . . has sense enough to value your present; for she is very fond of Stilton. Yours is the delicatest, rainbow-hued, melting piece I ever flavoured. |
| | Letter to Thomas Allsop, 1823 |

IN HISTORY

| **Hilaire Belloc** 1870-1953 | If antiquity be the only test of nobility, then cheese is a very noble thing . . . The lineage of cheese is demonstrably beyond all record. |
| | 'On Cheeses', *First and Last* |

| **Homer** fl. 900 B.C. | Polyphemus . . . quick did dress His half milk up for cheese, and in a press Of wicker press'd it; put in bowls the rest. |
| | *Odyssey*, trans. George Chapman |

DESIRED QUALITIES

| **Oswald Burdett** | Cheese, says Tusser, should not be 'whitish and dry' like Gehazi stricken with leprosy; nor 'too salt' like Lot's wife; nor full of eyes like Argus; nor 'hoven and puffed' like the cheeks of a piper; nor 'hairy' like Esau; nor full of whey or 'maudlin' like St Mary Magdalen; nor 'scrawling' with mites or gentils [maggots]; nor 'burnt to the pan' such as a maid, forgetting her curd to run out to watch a passing bishop, may unfairly curse him for having occasioned. |
| | *A Little Book of Cheese* (1935) |

| **Mrs Beeton** 1836-65 | Cream cheese, although so called, is not properly cheese but is nothing more than cream dried sufficiently to be cut with a knife. |
| | *A Book of Household Management* |

| **H. Rider Haggard** 1856-1925 | Mrs Musson of Wartnaby remarked that Stiltons, 'with the exception that they make no noise, are more trouble than babies'. |
| | *Rural England* |

TYPE CHARACTERISTICS

Evan Jones
T. A. Layton . . . described the smell [of Livarot] as 'like the odour of slowly rotting apples combined with ammonia, a whiff of ripe Camembert and a slight suggestion of seaside ozone.'
The World of Cheese (1976)

Marcella Hazan
There is no more magnificent table cheese than a piece of aged genuine *parmigiano-reggiano*, when it has not been allowed to dry out and it is a glistening, pale straw colour.
Classic Italian Cook Book

Edward Jones
The Cheshireman ran to his hold
And fetch'd a Cheshire cheese,
And said, Look here, you dog, behold!
We have such fruits as these.

Your fruits are ripe but twice a year,
As you yourself do say,
But such as I present you here
Our land brings twice a day.
A Cheshire Cheese Song (1786)

J. C. Jeafferson
Hunger will break through stone walls and anything except a Suffolk cheese. Suffolk, long infamous for its hard, horny fletmilk cheeses which Swift called 'cartwheels', and farm labourers designated 'bang' . . .
A Book about the Table (1875)

William Shakespeare
1564-1616
As thin as Banbury cheese.
The Merry Wives of Windsor

'Beachcomber' [J. B. Morton] 1893-1979
Loveliest of cheese, the Cheddar now . . .
Poem to a Shropshire Lad

H. A. Annesley Vachell
Cheddar is 'the cut and come again cheese. I commend it with all my heart'.
Cited by Evan Jones in *World of Cheese*

David Mabey

There's hardly a cheesemaker left in the Caer-philly area, but the Welsh still eat great quantities of the cheese from English and also Irish creameries.

In Search of Food (1978)

PROOF IN THE EATING

Anonymous

He smelt the cheese, and she smelt the cheese,
And they both pronounced it good;
And both remarked it would greatly add
To the charms of their daily food.

He and She

Jonathan Swift
1667-1745

'An off kind of fellow who, when the cheese came upon the table, pretended to faint; so somebody said, Pray, take away the cheese; No, said I, pray take away the fool . . . I wish we had a bit of your Lordship's Oxfordshire cheese.'

Polite Conversation

M. T. Braun

God of the country, bless today Thy cheese,
For which we give Thee thanks on bended knees.
Let them be fat or light, with onions blent,
Shallots, brine, pepper, honey; whether scent
Of sheep or fields is in them, in the yard,
Let them, good Lord, at dawn be beaten hard . . .
Whether from Parma or from Jura heights,
Kneaded by august hands of Carmelites,
Stamped with the mitre of a proud abbess,
Flowered with the perfumes of the grass of
    Bresse,
From hollow Holland, from the Vosges, from Brie,
From Roquefort, Gorgonzola, Italy!
Bless them, good Lord! Bless Stilton's royal fare,
Red Cheshire, and the tearful, cream Gryere.

Ode to Cheese, translated by Jethro Bithell

WHEN TO EAT

Brillat-Savarin
1755-1826

Dessert without cheese is like a beautiful woman with one eye.

Physiologie du Goût

Mrs: Pennell   Preposterous it would be truly to serve the mild-flavoured plebian species from Canada or America after a carefully ordered dinner. Port Salut, with its soothing suggestion of monastic peace, is a safeguard against indigestion.

Feasts of Autolycus (1896)

CHEESE MITES

Anonymous   The cheese-mites asked how the cheese got there,
And warmly debated the matter;
The orthodox said it came from the air,
And the Heretics said from the platter.

Notes and Queries

Oswald Burdett   Cheese-mites, the terror of vegetarians.

A Little Book of Cheese (1935)

COCOA

**Stanley J.
Sharpless**

*Lines written on hearing the startling news that cocoa is,
in fact, a mild aphrodisiac.*

Half past nine — high time for supper;
'Cocoa love?' 'Of course my dear.'
Helen thinks its quite delicious,
John prefers it now to beer.
Knocking back the sepia potion,
Hubby winks, says; 'Who's for bed?'
'Shan't be long,' says Helen softly,
Cheeks a faintly flushing red.
For they've stumbled on the secret
Of a love that never wanes,
Rapt beneath the tumbled bedclothes,
Cocoa coursing through their veins.

In Praise of Cocoa, Cupid's Nightcap

Brillat-Savarin
1755-1826

. . . let him be given a good pint of amber-flavour-
ed chocolate in the proportion of sixty to seventy-
two grains of amber to a pound, and marvels will
be performed . . .

Physiologie du Goût

Note: It is generally accepted today that what Brillat-
Savarin and Richelieu called 'amber' was actually
ambergris, a strongly-scented substance (once used in
perfume manufacture) from the intestines of the sperm
whale; and which was once thought to have
aphrodisiacal properties. *J.G.*

COFFEE

**William
Shakespeare**
1564-1616

. . . wouldst give me
Water with berries in't.

The Tempest (1612)

Note: Tannahill, in *Food in History*, says that 'only in
1610 did William Lithgow note that the people of
Constantinople made a hot beverage from a seed, and
that the first coffee house only opened in
Constantinople in 1554, which provokes the question,
'Was Shakespeare referring to coffee in *The Tempest*?'

Mauduit

In the making of coffee the French come first, then the Turks, then the Americans, while the English come sadly last on the list of 'also rans'.

The Vicomte in the Kitchen (1933)

Eliza Acton

We hear constant and well-founded complaints ... of the wretched compounds so commonly served up here [as coffee], especially in many lodging houses, hotels and railway refreshment rooms. At some of the principal stations ... the coffee is so bad that great as the refreshment of it would be to [travellers], ... they reject it as too nauseous to be swallowed ...

Modern Cookery for Private Families (1845)

W. M. Thackeray 1811-63

Why do they always put mud into coffee on board steamers? Why does the tea generally taste of boiled boots?

The Kicklebury's on the Rhine

Mark Twain 1835-1910

European coffee is an unknown beverage ... it resembles the real thing as hypocrisy resembles holiness. It is a feeble, characterless, uninspiring sort of stuff, and almost as undrinkable as if it had been made in an American hotel.

'European Diet', *A Tramp Abroad*

Alexander Pope 1688-1744

Coffee, which makes the politician wise
And see through all things with his half-shut eyes.

Anonymous

Here lies, cut down like unripe fruit,
The wife of Deacon Amos Shute.
She died of drinking too much coffee,
Anny Dominy, eighteen forty.

Epitaph from Connecticut

Lady Mary Wortley Montague 1689-1762

I went to the bagnio [Turkish bath] ... in the shape of a dome, but no windows but in the roof ... sofas were covered with cushions and rich carpets on which sat the ladies ... their slaves behind them, but without any distinction of rank, all being ... stark naked, without any beauty or defect concealed. Yet there was not the least wanton smile or immodest gesture ... to see so many fine women naked in different postures, some in

77

conversation, some working, others drinking coffee or sherbet, and many lying negligently on their cushions, while their slaves ... were braiding their hair ... In short it is the women's coffee house, where all the news of the town is told, scandal invented, etc.

Letter from Adrianople (Turkey), in *Letters*

COFFEE ESPRESSO

Christopher Driver

Many young people ... were in 1955 still to be found in coffee bars ... normally run by Italian caterers ... on the strength of the machine that had been invented by Achille Gaggia in 1946 ... There were far more espresso machines installed in London than there were ever Italian engineers to maintain them. Typically, operators ran them until they seized up with their own sludge: British coffee returned to its weak norm or succumbed to the instant substitute, and restaurateurs found it easier to amuse their customers with hour-glass Cona devices ... a fool-proof coffee-making device has yet to be invented, and may never be, since the British market is the only one that stands in need of it.

The British at Table 1940-1980 (1983)

CURDS AND WHEY

Anonymous   Little Miss Muffet
Sat on a tuffet
Eating her curds and whey.
  Nursery rhyme

Susan Ogilvy   When milk becomes acid or rennet is added . . .
the milk becomes junket-like . . . forming a curd
. . . rennet curd is the basis of most hard and soft
cheeses. Acid curd is used for acid curd cheeses,
yoghurt and other cultured-milk products.
  Curds and Whey (1979)

DAMPER

Mrs Charles   I think it the worst way of spoiling flour . . . this
Meredith   indigestible food being supposed . . . to have been
1812-95   invented by the great circumnavigator [Dampier]
. . . When cut into, it exceeds in closeness and
hard heaviness the worst bread or pudding I ever
tasted and the outside looks dirty . . . In 'the bush',
where brewer's yeast cannot be procured, or people are too idle or too ignorant to manufacture a
substitute for it (which is easily done); this in-
durate dough is the only kind of bread used, and
those who eat it must have an ostrich's digestion . . .
  Notes and Sketches of New South Wales (1844)

Anonymous   The babbling brook*
The shovel took
The damper to unfold.
'Another sod?
So help me God
That beats the flamin' world'.
  Old Bush ballad, cited in *Bill Harney Cook Book* (1960)
  *Rhyming slang for 'cook'

Bill Harney   When Cliff Lynott, a storekeeper at Borroloola . . .
found that Eno's Fruit Salts made a damper rise
beautifully . . . he sent a testimonial to Eno's fac-
tory in England, telling them that their Salts were
in great demand in the Australian outback for

bread-making. He was amazed when he never
got a reply.

Bill Harney Cook Book (1960)

Charles Sturt   I watch the distorted countenances of my humble
companions while drinking their tea and eating
their damper.

Southern Australia (1833)

DUMPLINGS

Charles Lamb   C[oleridge] . . . holds that a man cannot have a
1775-1834   pure mind who refuses apple-dumplings. I am not
certain but he is right.

'Grace Before Meat', *Essays of Elia*

Carol Willson   In Salzburg . . . what staggered us was not the
and John Goode   delicious food we ordered but the dumplings. On
each plate there sat a baseball-sized dumpling. We
weren't sure whether or not they were for eating
or for bowling at the cook if his game displeased
us!

'*Fahrten* through Europe', *Epicurean*

FRUMENTY

Susan Ogilvy   Frumenty . . . is made from whole wheat, boiled
until it is swollen and soft and then mixed with
cream, spices, currants, egg yolks and brandy. It
can probably claim to be our [English] oldest dish,
going back to Neolothic farmers who boiled their
rough-ground wheat to make primitive pottages
and gruels.

Curds and Whey (1979)

FISH SOUP

Jean Hewitt   One thing common to all New England clam-
bakes is chowder . . . and rarely with tomatoes . . .
no milk or cream is added . . . The liquid is clam
broth and water, and the solids . . . fried salt pork
pieces, a little onion, diced potatoes, and chopped
. . . hard-shelled clams.

New England Heritage Cookbook (1979)

Norman Douglas
1868-1952

Take breath, gentle maiden; the while I explain ... the ingredients of the diabolical preparation known as *zuppa di pesce*. The guarracino, ... a pitch black, marine monstrosity, one or two *inches* long ... As to the *scorfano*, its name is unquestionably onomatopoeic, to suggest the spitting-out of bones ... The *aguglia*, is thin as a lead pencil ... [for] this miserable sea worm, with verdigris-tinted spine, the inhabitants of Siren land fought like fiends ... And everybody knows the *totero* or squid, an animated ink-bag of perverse leanings ... whose indiarubber flesh might be useful for deluding hunger on desert islands, since, like American gum, you can chew it for months but never get it down. These and such as they, float about in a lukewarm brew of rancid oil and garlic, together with a few of last week's breadcrusts, decaying sea-shells and onion-peels ... This is the stuff for which Neapolitans sell their female relatives.

Siren Land (1911)

Marika Hanbury Tenison

Bouillabaisse, or fish soup, is also considered to be the prerogative of the French, yet fish soups have been popular around the coasts of Britain for centuries.

The Best of British Cooking (1976)

GRAVY

Sydney Smith
1771-1845

Madam, I have been looking for a person who disliked gravy all my life.

Lady Holland's *Memoir*

Elizabeth Ray

When is a gravy not a sauce? At the present time, 'gravy' is either the plain meat juice or something from a cube or bottle, and anything more elaborate becomes a 'sauce'.

The Best of Eliza Acton (1974)

Derek Cooper

... the British ... [are] partial to pouring gravy over everything, especially when it has the consistency of heavy-duty engine oil ...

The Bad Food Guide (1967)

British . . . gravy . . . has the consistency of heavy duty engine oil.

HOT CROSS BUNS

Anonymous

One a penny, two a penny, hot cross buns.
> Old street cry, cited by Henry Mayhew in *London Labour and the London Poor* (1851)

Philippa Pullar

Hot cross buns, it is believed, date from the time [of Pope Gregory I, about A.D. 600]. They were originally cakes eaten by the Anglo-Saxons in honour of the goddess Eastre, which the clergy . . . exorcised and marked with a cross.
> *Consuming Passions* (1970)

John Strype (ed.)

That no bakers . . . make, utter, or sell by retail . . . any spice cakes, buns, biscuits, or other . . . except it be at burials, or on the Friday before Easter, or at Christmas, upon pain or forfeiture of all such spiced bread to the poor.
> *Stow's Survey of London* (1598)

Elizabeth David

In the time of James I, further attempts to prevent bakers from making spiced breads and buns proved impossible, and . . . were allowed.
> *English Bread and Yeast Cookery* (1977)

Allan Jobson	One for the poker,
Two for the tongs;
Three for the dust-pan,
Hot Cross Buns.
An Hour-glass on the Run (1959)

JOHNNY CAKES

Bill Harney	In the Australian bush, small dampers made about
as big as the palm of your hand, and patted very
thin . . .
Bill Harney Cookbook (1960)

Rachel Henning	Tom lit a great fire and made some beautiful
'johnny cakes' — thin soda cakes which are baked
in about ten minutes and are the best bread that
you ever ate.
Letters written in 1862, ed. D. Adams (1963)

LEATHERJACKETS

S. Mossman &	Our party . . . indulged themselves . . . with what
T. Bannister	are called 'Leather jackets', an Australian bush
term for a thin cake made of dough and put into a
pan to bake with some fat . . . The Americans . . .
giving them the name of 'Puff ballooners', the
only difference being that they place the cake
upon the bare coals.
Australia Visited and Revisited (1853)

Henry Lawson	I wish I had just enough fat to make the pan siss;
1867-1922	I'd treat myself to a leather-jacket; but it took
three weeks' skimmin' to get enough of them
theer doughboys.
Prose

MACARONI

Ambrose Bierce	An Italian food made in the form of a slender,
1842-c.1914	hollow tube. It consists of two parts — the tubing
and the hole, the latter being the part that digests.
The Enlarged Devil's Dictionary

Giuseppe Tomasi di Lampedusa

... the aspect of those monumental dishes of macaroni was worthy of the quivers of admiration they evoked. The burnished gold of the crusts, the fragrance of sugar and cinnamon they exuded, were but the preludes to the delights released from the interior when the knife broke the crust; first came a spice-laden haze, then chicken livers, hard-boiled eggs, sliced ham, chicken and truffles in masses of piping hot, glistening macaroni to which the meat juice gave an exquisite hue of suede.

The Leopard (1960)

Boccaccio
c.1313-75

At Bengodi (in the province of Parma) 'there is a mountain consisting entirely of Parmesan cheese ... on which live people who do nothing but make maccheroni and ravioli, and cook it in capon broth'.

Cited by Elizabeth David in *Italian Food* (1963)

MILK

Thomas Fuller
1654-1734

Who'd keep a cow when he may have a quart of milk for a penny.

Gnomologia

BUT NOT QUITE ...

Mark Twain
1835-1910

... what the French call 'Christian' milk — milk which has been baptised.

'European Diet', *A Tramp Abroad*

W. S. Gilbert
1836-1911

Things are never what they seem,
Skim milk masquerades as cream.

H.M.S. Pinafore

John Ray
1628-1705

If you would live forever
You must wash milk from your liver.

English Proverbs

MUFFINS

G. Bernard Shaw
1856-1950

... at the end of the week you'll find no more
inspiration in her than in a plate of muffins.
Man and Superman II

T. F. Garrett

... it is customary to associate muffins with
crumpets ... both are made of batter, both require
re-cooking, and both are served hot and well-but-
tered; yet there is so marked a difference between
the two in flavour and constitution that most persons have a decided preference for one or the
other.
The Encyclopaedia of Practical Cookery (1899)

OATS AND OATMEAL

Samuel Johnson
1709-84

Oats: A grain, which in England is generally given
to horses, but in Scotland supports the people.
Dictionary of the English Language

David Mabey

It is actually the oatmeal ... obtained after the
oats have been ground and the husks removed —
which provides the basis of so many Scottish
foods. Oatmeal comes in three grades — fine, medium and coarse ... Fine ... goes into dough;
herrings are floured in it before cooking, and it is
the basis for some bannocks ... and scones. Medium ... it is used for bannocks, and for oatcakes,
and for mixing with meat dishes.
In Search of Food (1978)

Sydney Smith
1771-1845

The motto I proposed for the [Edinburgh] *Review*
was 'Tenui musam meditamur avena' [We culti-
vate literature on a little oatmeal]; but this was too
near the truth to be admitted ...
Cited in Lady Holland's *Memoir*

Anonymous

A herring fried in nutty oatmeal and accompanied
by a mustard sauce ... makes a noble supper dish,
and never better than when coarse oatmeal is
used and the fish fried in bacon fat. For brown

trout ... a dusting of the finest oatmeal ...
cooked in butter.

Cited by F. Marian McNeill, in *The Scots Kitchen*
(1929)

PASTA

‽Marinetti Futurist cooking will be liberated from the ancient
obsession of weight and volume and one of its
principal aims will be the abolition of *pastaciutta*
... an obsolete food; it is heavy, brutalising and
gross; its nutritive qualities are deceptive; it induces scepticism, sloth and pessimism.

Italian futurist poet's Manifesto, uttered in Milan, 15
November 1930

Duke of Bovino, The angels in Paradise eat nothing but *vermicelli al*
Mayor of Naples *pomidoro*.

In answer to Marinetti, 1930.

Alexandre Macaroni was brought to France by the Floren-
Dumas tines, probably at the time when Catherine de
1802-70 Medici came to marry Henry II ... semolina is
converted into dough, pounded and crushed and
put in a metal cylinder surrounded by a heating
apparatus. At the bottom of the cylinder is a sort
of sieve, pierced with little slits of the same size as
one wants the strips of macaroni to assume. By
means of pressure, the dough is forced out of this
mould.

Dumas on Food, translated by Alan and Jane Davidson
(1979)

Note: In 1982 there was a village, north of Chiangmai in
northern Thailand, devoted wholly to the making of
rice noodles. Rice flour was made into a thin dough and
put into forcing bags with perforated metal ends. The
paste was forced through the screen into pots of boiling
water, where it cooked for about three minutes before
being fished out with a bamboo basket and then dipped
into cold water, before draining. All rice noodles were
sold next morning in Chiangmai, in a sloppy form for
heating and eating that day. *J.G.*

Merry White Among the 'myths of origin', the most popular
[concerning pasta] revolves around Marco Polo's

trip to the Orient in the 1270s ... Yet the existence of the noodle in Italy predated his trip, for rules governing the size and shape of noodles existed there as early as 1200.

Noodles Galore (1976)

Irene Rooney

The Spaghetti Historical Museum in Pontedassio ... [a] tiny Mediterranean village near the French border ... [offers] visible proof that as far back as Etruscan times, some 500 years B.C., Italy's ancient race had all the standard equipment for making pasta.

A thousand years before Marco Polo's epic journey, Apicio Celio, head chef to Emperor Tiberius, was stoking his master's appetite with a type of spaghetti ... There are nearly 300 different types [of pasta] in all sizes, shapes and weights.

'It's a World of Spaghetti', *Sun-Herald*

PASTRY

Eliza Acton

In mixing paste ... it should be lightly kneaded until it is as smooth as possible. When carelessly made, the surface is often left covered with small dry crumbs or lumps ...

Modern Cookery (1845)

Jonathan Swift
1667-1745

Promises and pie-crust are made to be broken.

Polite Conversation

Anne Marshall

One of the earliest ... was a simple flour and water paste, called 'huff paste', which was used to wrap around ham and poultry to keep the juices in during baking ... fat was added to this paste to make it more pliable ... choux is named after the French for cabbage because it puffs out like one when baked.

Anne's Perfect Piebook (1979)

'Bon Viveur'
[John and Fanny
Cradock]

Pastry prefers to remain aloof. It bitterly resents being stroked and patted. Such treatment makes it ... settle into a leaden sulk. Baking powder only gives it violent indigestion and successfully ruins flavour and texture too.

The Daily Telegraph Cook's Book (1964)

PORRIDGE

David Mabey
Outside Scotland [porridge] is often made without care, and becomes a lumpy, cloying sludge. It should be made with medium oatmeal simmered in water with a little salt added to it ... When ready, the porridge is dished into cold bowls and a small dish of cold milk is provided. Each spoonful of hot porridge is dipped into the cold milk before being eaten ... [it] is normally seasoned with extra salt though many people prefer sugar or even treacle. One of the most fortifying winter breakfasts I have ever eaten consisted of a bowl of porridge generously laced with malt whisky.

In Search of Food (1978)

John Phoenix
The man in the Moon, came down too soon
To inquire the way to Norwich;
The man in the South, he burned his mouth,
Eating cold, hot porridge.

Cited in 'Lectures on Astronomy' in *Phoenixiana*
(c.1880)

'Cassandra'
[William
Connor]
... If ever a word describing food had the sound of its meaning, it is 'Porridge' — the slup and slur and costive slirrup of the uneatable ... How I remember that lake of oatmeal slime ... a glutinous sea of salt and milk and coarse oats all sludged together under the Calvinistic battle cry of 'It will do you good and make you grow up into a big boy'.

'Miss Cowie's Porridge', *Daily Mirror* (1961)

Elizabeth Craig
To make [porridge] in the old-fashioned way, you should stir them with a porridge stick sometimes called a spurtle, sometimes a theevil. In bygone days, every girl had at least one theevil in her bottom drawer. I had three.

The Scottish Cookery Book (1956)

RICE

Confucius
c.550-478 B.C.
Rice must be polished, cleaned and washed before cooking.

Cited in *Royal Cookbook* (1971)

Laurens van der Post	One of the main reasons for trying to get back to Zanzibar was to try to rescue this form of rice from oblivion . . . a version of what is called celo rice in Persia (Iran) . . . a dish out of the tale of a thousand and one nights . . . five elements were of fundamental importance . . . patience, time . . . you could not do the dish in less than twelve hours — rice consisting only of unblemished grains, water with a considerable content of chalk and a wood fire.

First Catch your Eland (1977)

Trevor Wilson	Rice may be associated with Oriental dishes, but it took some folk genius of the Western world to discover that if you add raw rice to a casserole or rich stew . . . in doing this it will become impregnated with all the flavours and aromas of the other ingredients. This discovery resulted in some of the world's finest national dishes — risottos, paellas, pilafs, dolmades — coming from the countries bordering the Mediterranean . . .

Great Rice Dishes of the World (1970)

A. A. Milne 1882-1956	*What* is the matter with Mary Jane? She's perfectly well and she hasn't a pain, *And it's lovely rice pudding for dinner again* . . .

'Rice Pudding', *When We Were Very Young*

SALAD DRESSING

Ogden Nash 1902-71	A dressing is not a compôte A dressing is not a custard It consists of pepper and salt, Vinegar, oil and mustard.

'O! The Chef has Imagination', *The Private Dining Room* . . .

Abraham Hayward 1801-84	According to the Spanish proverb, four persons are wanted to make a good salad [dressing]: a spendthrift for oil, a miser for vinegar, a counsellor for salt and a madman to stir it all up.

The Art of Dining

SAUCES

Simone Beck,
Louisette
Bertholle
& Julia Child

Sauces are the splendour and glory of French cooking.

Mastering the Art of French Cooking (1961)

Anonymous

... paradox of the *grandes sauces* of French cooking [is that] their basic processes are all foreign imports — the roux from Spain, the Hollandaise from the Low Countries, and the Mayonnaise ... from common Mediterranean practice. The all-important ingredient which France added to all of them was simply imagination.

Posthumous Introduction to Ambrose Heath, *The Penguin Book of Sauces* (1970)

J. R. Lowell
1819-91

Of all the sarse that I can call to mind,
England doos the most onpleasant kind ...

The Biglow Papers

Anonymous

I detect the hand of an artist: the shredded lamb, the chick peas, the pine kernels; the cardamom seeds; the nutmeg; the cloves; the ginger; the pepper; and the various aromatic herbs. I taste them as a whole, and I taste them separately, so exquisite is the blending.

Cited without source by Leyell and Hartley, *The Gentle Art of Cookery* (1925)

Stephen Watts

... it is the sauce, says M. [Charles] Ritz, which sells the fish.

The Ritz (1963)

Derek Cooper

Sauces are greatly admired by the British. We like tomato sauce ... bottled mint sauce, which often tastes like vinegarized straw and is coloured a brilliant green like a traffic light ... we like our sauces to come to the table in the bottle so that in between examining the other guests we can read the labels and memorize the lists of ingredients.

The Bad Food Guide (1967)

SCOTCH BROTH

'Cassandra' [William Connor]

Scotch Broth . . . is almost a compulsory dish. I do not care for it, and I class it as an admonitory soup. It is an imprecatory soup, and it carries with it that ominous warning, so often applied to many unappetising dishes, that 'It is good for you'.

'Scotch Broth', *Daily Mirror* (1961)

. . . SHOES AND SHIPS

Nowadays the term 'hushpuppy' is better known in Australia and parts of the USA as a brand of shoe. The original Hush Puppies were somewhat different.

Lila Perl

On fishing and hunting trips, a sack of cornmeal was taken to make little balls of corn-pone which were fried in the fat right along with the fish. As the hot crusty balls browned . . . they gave off such a delicious odour that the hunting dogs . . . began to whine . . . To quiet the pleading hounds, the fishermen or huntsmen would toss them some of the savoury fried cornmeal pones with the words, 'Hush, puppy'.

Slumps, Grunts and Snickerdoodles (1975)

'SINKER'

Bill Harney

[Use] the same basic dough [as a damper] in rounds about the size of a tennis ball. Put them into the boiling stewpot . . . with a bit of fat on top which helps to seal the dough . . . usually served hot with golden syrup.

Bill Harney Cook Book (1960)

SOUP

Mauduit

Soup is the time-honoured dish of the peasants, traditional in every part of the world . . . France has the pot-au-feu . . . and the *Garbure* in the

Basque country, England has turtle and oxtail soups, Scotland the Scotch Broth, Italy the *Minestrone*, Spain the *Puchero*, Holland the *Erwtensoep*, Russia the *Borshtch*, America the *Clam-chowder* and everywhere the Rossolnick*, the most expensive soup in the world.

* His recipe in French uses the term *argousis*, that is in no dictionary available. However, other sources in English describe *potage Rossolnick* as basically a cucumber-flavoured chicken soup! Obviously one of the Viscount's little jokes! *J.G.*

The Vicomte in the Kitchen (1933)

Reay Tannahill

... though the average Greek was no great gourmet, even he shuddered at the diet favoured by the Spartans, whose black broth — reputedly made of pork stock, vinegar and salt — was infamous ... Athanaeus ... said 'It is natural enough for Spartans to be the bravest of men; for any man in his senses would rather die a thousand times over than live as miserably as this'.

The Fine Art of Food (1968)

'Saki' [H. H. Munro]
1870-1916

I believe that I once considerably scandalised her by declaring that clear soup was a more important factor in life than a clear conscience.

The Blind Spot

Frank Harris
1855-1931

'Why do you leave that?' he exclaimed, pointing to the pieces of green meat on my plate ... 'Is that what you call Calipash?' I asked, pointing with a smile to the green gobbets on my plate.

'Of course,' he said, 'they used to give you Calipash and Calipee with every plateful [of turtle soup] ... Eat that up,' he said ... 'it'll go to your ribs and make a man of you. I gained three pounds at my first Banquet ...'

My Life and Loves

REGIONAL VARIATIONS

'Cassandra' [William Connor]

... At Boulou, near the Pyrenees, I came across a magnificent soup of strong Spanish extraction ... a symphonic soup — a gastronomic tone poem ... a truly princely soup, best eaten to the sound of castanets. It is substantial but not filling, intriguing but not impertinent; bold but not blatant. And saffron provides a haunting theme; indescribable but inescapable.

'The Singing Soups of Spain', *Daily Mirror* (1957)

Anthony A. Scott

The most characteristic soup [of the Vilna district of Poland] is Borsch. Made from beetroot ... it is served in both thick and clear forms. A raw egg is served with the clear variety, and the eater places the [raw] egg in hot soup and beats it up, when it cooks and forms a floating flaky solid ... in this excellent soup, the earthy taste of beetroot is delicious, and its colour has the beauty of a fine claret.

'Gastronomy in Vilna', *We shall Eat and Drink Again* (c.1943)

HISTORIC

Susan Ogilvy

The earliest soups were the thick, cereal-based pottages ... to the basic brew were added seeds, leaves, roots of wild plants, fruits, nuts and pulses ... through the Middle Ages pottage was still enjoyed by all classes of people: the oatmeal porridge of the north, the rice pottage of the rich made with almonds and spices as an accompaniment to meat, the barley frumenty of the poor and the pease pottage, served with bacon for the gentry and without for the peasant's family. But by the end of the seventeenth century ... a thin pottage began to be served on its own as a first course and was known as 'soupe'.

Curds and Whey (1979)

STILTON

Oswald Burdett

Stilton ... derives its name from the village in Huntingdonshire where, at the Bell Inn, it was first sold in the last decade of the eighteenth century by its inventor's [Mrs Paulet] kinsman Cooper Thornhill.

A Little Book of Cheese (1935)

David Mabey   Quenby Hall where 'Lady Beaumont's Cheese' was being made at the beginning of the 18th century ... seems to have been the true ancestor of Stilton. One of the daughters of ... the Quenby Housekeeper married Cooper Thornhill and cheeses were sent there by her sister, Mrs Paulet, from Wymondham, near Melton Mowbray ... To be called Stilton, the cheese has to be made in its traditional regions: the vale of Belvoir in Leicestershire, and parts of south Nottinghamshire.

In Search of Food (1978)

John Squire   I should no more want Stilton on a hot day than I should want boiled silverside and dumplings. Stilton is essentially ... for cold months, when appetites are robust and in want of warming up.

Cheddar Gorge: A Book of English Cheeses (1937)

TEA

G. K. Chesterton
1874-1936

Tea, though an oriental
Is a gentleman at least;
Cocoa is a cad and coward,
Cocoa is a vulgar beast.

The Song of Right and Wrong

John Masefield
1878-1967

Oh, some are fond of Spanish wine and some are fond of French,
And some'll swallow tay and stuff fit only for a wench.

Captain Stratton's Fancy

ITS INFLUENCE

Colley Cibber
1671-1757

Tea! thou soft, thou sober, sage and venerable liquid ... thou female tongue-running, smile-toothing, heart opening, wink-tippling cordial, to whose glorious insipidity I owe the happiest moments of my life, let me fall prostrate ...

The Lady's Last Stake

Alexander Pope
1688-1744

Here, thou, great Anna! whom three realms obey,
Dost sometimes counsel take — and sometimes Tea.

The Rape of the Lock

William Cowper
1731-1800

... while the bubbling and loud-hissing urn
Throws up a steamy column, the cups
That cheer but not inebriate, wait on each ...
The Task

Sydney Smith
1771-1845

Thank God for tea! What would the world do
without tea?
How did it exist? I am glad I was not born before
tea.
Lady Holland's *Memoir* I

James Joyce
1882-1941

When I makes tea I makes tea, as old mother
Grogan said. And when I makes water I makes
water ... Begob, ma'am, says Mrs Cahill, God
send you don't make them in the one pot.
Ulysses

**Thomas De
Quincy**
1785-1859

Tea, though ridiculed by those who are naturally
coarse in their nervous sensibilities ... will always be the favourite beverage of the intellectual.
Confessions of an English Opium-Eater

TOAST

James Payn
1830-98

I never have a piece of toast
Particularly long and wide
But fell upon the sanded floor,
And always on the buttered side.

Chambers Journal (1884)

Dorris McFerran Townsend

When you were sick as a child, were you fed milk toast?
Remember how it steamed, how the butter melted into little rivulets?

The Cook's Companion (1978)

WATER

Andrew Boorde

Water [is] not wholesome, bad for Englysche men, colde, slow, slack of digestion.

Dietary of Helthe (1542?)

Sir George Reid

Never have I seen so much enthusiasm for water — and so little of it drunk.

At opening of Goldfields Water Scheme, to serve Western Australian desert gold mining towns, in 1902

Horace
65-8 B.C.

No verses can please long, or live, which are written by water drinkers.

Epistles

A. E. Housman
1859-1936

He drank like a fish, if drinking nothing but water could be so described.

Letters

Charles Neaves
1800-76

I'm very fond of water;
It ever must delight
Each mother's son and daughter,
When qualified aright.

'I'm very fond of Water'

WHEAT

Anonymous
'I don't know what you call plump wheat, but there are seventeen in our family ... and when we want bread we just go out and fetch in a kernel of wheat and bake it.'
'Do you ever soak it in water first?'
'Oh, no; that wouldn't do. It would swell a little, and then we couldn't get it in our range oven.'

'Minnesota Wheat' in *Mark Twain's Library of Humour* (1888)

YOGHURT

Sonia Uvezian
Yogurt is a basic food in the Caucasus ... That made from water buffalo is richer and sweeter. Yogurt is eaten plain, diluted with water to make a refreshing beverage, used as a base for soups, sauces, and salads, and even made into butter and cheese.

The Best Foods of Russia (1976)

Claudia Roden
In every Middle Eastern household, the making of yoghourt is ... a creative ritual which gives satisfaction similar to that of planting a seed and watching it grow ... [It] is an essential part of the ... diet. In al-Baghdadi's medieval manual it was referred to as 'Persian milk' ... as in the Balkans, yoghourt is believed by some people to have medicinal and therapeutic qualities — longevity and a strong constitution are sometimes attributed to the daily consumption ...

A Book of Middle Eastern Food (1968)

YORKSHIRE PUDDING

Ogden Nash
1902-71
Let us call Yorkshire pudding
A fortunate blunder;
It's a sort of popover
That's tripped and popped under.

'Yorkshire Pudding'

David Mabey ... flour, egg and milk beaten together was put beneath a joint of roasting meat to absorb the juices ... traditionally the pudding was eaten with any kind of roast meat in Yorkshire, from beef to rabbit or partridge ... or served as a kind of first course, eaten on its own with thick gravy ... the beauty is that it has two distinct parts ... inside pieces ... [were] moist and saturated with the juices from the joint ... the outside, in contact with the sides of the baking tin, were light, brown and crisp. The trick was to ensure that you obtained pieces from both parts ...

In Search of Food (1978)

FRUITS OF THE EARTH

APPLES

Thomas Hood
1799-1845

When Eve upon the first of men
The apple press'd with specious cant,
Oh! What a thousand pitties then
That Adam was not adamant.
A Reflection

Thomas Cogan
1545?-1607

Apples are thought to quench the flame of
Venus . . .
He that will not a wife wed
Must eat cold apple when he goeth to bed
Though some turn it to a contrary purpose.
Haven of Health (1588)

Peter Wynne

Pliny . . . writes of a Syrian red apple . . . called
orthomastion, meaning 'upturned breast' in
Greek because it was thought to resemble a
woman's bosom . . . The ancient Greeks called
breasts 'apples', as do modern Russians (although
the latter use is considered vulgar). Perhaps, then,
one reason Aphrodite had a soft spot for the apple
might have been that it is shaped like a woman's
breast and that both the apple and the breast
provide sustenance.
Apples (1975)

Anonymous

Lovers [in the time of Horace] customarily
squeezed apple seeds between their first two fingers, shooting them at the ceiling and thus augur-
ing whether they could hope to realise their
dreams.

The apple tree replaced the maypole, that ancient phallic symbol, after it had been banned by
the Puritans in the seventeenth century.
Cited by Wynne, op. cit.

Anonymous If you can break an apple in half with your hands, you will always be your own boss.

Kentucky superstition

ARTICHOKES

Eliza Acton ... artichokes, which are said to be improved by
1799-1859 two or three days' keeping.

Modern Cooking for Private Families (1845)

Edith Templeton ... the artichoke is not a suitable meal for the businessman or the salesgirl. It is by nature inaccessible to him who is used to cutting up his greens, shovelling them on the fork together with meat and potatoes and swallowing in haste.

The Surprise of Cremona (n.d.)

Andre Launay The artichoke is, after all, an extremely civilised thistle with a very gastronomic beginning. Not to be confused with the globe artichoke is the Jerusalem artichoke or Topinambour ... [they] are warty, unattractive, potato-like tubers which taste sweet ...

Caviare and After (1946)

Yann Lovelock ... an Italian novel of the fifteenth century mentioned it as an aphrodisiac 'dear to Venus'. Perhaps it was this that fed the great sexual appetite of Catherine of Medici ... who was very fond of it; so too was England's much married Henry VIII.

The Vegetable Book: An unnatural history (1972)

ASPARAGUS

Joel Chandler Hit look lak sparrer-grass, hit feel lak sparrer-
Harris grass,
1848-1908 hit tas'e lak sparrer-grass, en I bless ef'taint sparrer-grass.

Nights with Uncle Remus

Andre Launay	In asparagus there are traces of sulphur which, though not immediately detectable to the olfactory senses, are strong enough to ruin a wine, unless the asparagus is served as a garnish, or with grated cheese. Wines therefore should be avoided.
	Caviare and After (1964)
Alexis Soyer 1809-58	The Romans cultivated this plant with extreme care ... At Ravenna [Pliny claimed] they raised asparagus, each stem of which weighed three pounds [1.36 kg] ... they chose the finest heads ... and dried them. When wanted ... they boiled them a few minutes ... Connoisseurs had it brought from Nesia, a city of Campania.
	Pantropheon (1853)
Augustus 63 B.C.-A.D. 14	Let that be done quicker than you would cook asparagus.
	In Suetonius, *Lives of the Caesars: Augustus*
Bill Rathje	With fresh asparagus, the higher your income the higher up the stalk you cut off the tip.
	Results of his research, as Professor at University of Arizona, from sifting household rubbish, as a guide to social behaviour (1985)

AVOCADO

Doris McFerran Townsend	If this page could be wired for sound, it would be so that the praises of the glorious avocado could be appropriately set to music ... [It] was served to Hernando Cortez ... by Montezuma at Tenochtitlan, now Mexico City, in 1519. In Chile, Peru and Ecuador ... known as *palta* ... the rough skin of some varieties responsible for the name 'alligator pear'.
	The Cook's Companion (1978)
Diana Kennedy	... watery Florida avocados (all right for slicing and garnishing but not for making rich sauces or guacamole) instead of creamy ones from California.
	Recipes from Regional Cooks of Mexico (1978)

BANANAS

Frank Silver and Irving Cohn

Yes we have no bananas
We have no bananas today.

Yes, We Have No Bananas (song of 1923)

Anonymous

The banana does not bear twice (Once bitten, twice shy).

Malay proverb

Bernard Levin

I cannot get it out of my head that when I peel a banana, if I do not, before eating it, remove also the fine string threads . . . I shall contract leprosy.

'Like the arts, good food and drink has its place', *Enthusiasms* (1984)

BAOBAB

Laurens van der Post

We called [the baobab] 'cream of tartar' tree, because from the seeds of its fruit we made a crude kind of baking powder . . . we used the fruit, too, as people still do in the far west of Africa. Dried, it made a welcome addition to our cooking. On . . . hot and rainless days I placed baobab seeds underneath my tongue to let the astringent tartar . . . keep my thirst away.

First Catch Your Eland (1977)

BEANS, DRIED

Anonymous

Beans, beans, the musical fruit,
The more you eat, the more you toot.

Shake a Leicestershire yeoman by the collar
And you shall hear beans rattle in his belly.
Shake a Leicestershire woman by the petticoat
And the beans will rattle in her throat.

Cited by Robert Charles in *Foodmanship* (1977)

Craig and Ann Sams

Pythagoras would not let his students eat beans . . . because the prevalent bean of classical Greece was the fava — harmless in itself but with a hard brown skin which, if regularly eaten can lead to favism ... deterioration of vision and mental faculties.

The Brown Rice Cookbook (1980)

J. C. Bassidy
1860-1928

I come from the city of Boston,
The home of the bean and the cod,
Where the Cabots talk only to Lowells
And Lowells speak only to God.

On the Aristocracy of Harvard

Anonymous

Every pease has its vease (fart)
But every bean fifteen.

Traditional English adage, cited by Lovelock in *The Vegetable Book*

BEETROOT

Anthony A. Scott

... a vegetable ... usually found in England plainly boiled as an accompaniment of cold meat and in salads and hors d'oeuvres ... The sight of slabs or cubes of cold boiled beetroot makes me feel rather ill, probably because it used to be the inevitable accompaniment of stringy cold beef in my early schooldays, its vinegary, crimson liquor staining and spoiling the mashed potatoes.

'Gastronomy in Vilna', *We Shall Eat and Drink Again* (c.1943)

BERRIES

Viherjuuri, M., Tanttu, A-M and J.

Later on the strawberry is joined by wild strawberries, blueberries from the forests and black and red currants from one's own bushes, cloudberries, raspberries, lingonberries and cranberries ... One of the greatest pleasures in summer is to go out picking berries in the forest, which for many Finns is just a few steps from home. The aroma of the berries is captured in home-made jams — but also in industrially produced goods such as liqueurs.

Finlandia Gastronomica (1974)

CABBAGE

Ambrose Bierce
1842-c.1914

Cabbage: a familiar kitchen-garden vegetable about as large and wise as a man's head.

    The Devil's Dictionary

Juvenal
fl. 60-120

Like warmed-up cabbage served at each repast,
The repetition kills the wretch at last.

    Satires

Athenaeus
fl. c.200

The ancient Egyptians are the only people among whom it was a custom at their feasts to eat boiled cabbages before all the rest of their food.

    Cited in *The Deipnosophists* (1927)

**Maria
Edgeworth**
1767-1849

So she went into the garden to cut a cabbage leaf, to make an apple pie.

    Harry and Lucy Concluded

Lewis Carroll
1832-1898

Of shoes — and ships — and sealing wax —
Of cabbages — and kings . . .

    Through the Looking Glass

**'Cassandra'
[William
Connor]**

Boiled cabbage *à l'Anglaise* is something compared with which steamed coarse newsprint bought from bankrupt Finnish salvage dealers and heated over smoky oil stoves is an exquisite delicacy.

    'How I like my cabbage', *Daily Mirror* (1950)

CAPERS

Ben Jonson
1572-1637

Yet shall you have to rectify your palate,
An olive, capers or some better salad.

    Epigrams

CARROTS

Anonymous

Honey underground
Is the winter carrot
Between St Andrew's Day and Christmas.

    Old Gaelic rhyme, cited in *The Scots Kitchen* (1929)

CELERY

Marika Hanbury Tenison

Part of the fun [with] celery used to be that it appeared only during the winter ... and was so fresh and full of flavour. Now it seems to be around all the year ... from as far away as Spain and California (places one would have sworn never had the all-important frost which gives celery that crunchy texture) and all too often it is flaccid and tasteless.

The Best of British Cooking (1976)

CHARD

Grimod de la Reynière

... the *ne plus ultra* of human skill, and a cook capable of preparing a plate of chard to perfection has the right to call himself the finest artist in Europe.

Almanachs des Gourmands (1803-10)

CRESS

John Grange
fl. 1577

Eat well of the cress.
The Golden Aphroditis

Note: Cress was supposed to help the memory.

CUCUMBER

R. H. Barham
1788-1845

'Tis not *her* coldness, father,
That chills my labouring breast;
It's that confounded cucumber
I've ate and can't digest.
'The Confession'

James Boswell
1740-95

Dr Johnson told me that Gay's line in the *Beggar's Opera*, 'As men should serve a cucumber, etc.' has no waggish meaning, with reference to men flinging away cucumbers as too *cooling*, which some have thought; for it has been a common saying of physicians in England, that a cucumber should be well sliced, and dressed with pepper and vinegar, and then thrown out, as good for nothing.

The Journal of a Tour to the Hebrides with Samuel Johnson LL.D. 1773

Note: In Japan, a cucumber is always pre-prepared by making slits or grooves along its length and filling them with salt. This extracts much of the water and makes them much more digestible. The salt is washed off before serving. *J.G.*

DATES

Reay Tannahill
In some regions, the date palm has flourished as far back as 50,000 B.C. ... it is said to have 360 different uses. Even the stones can be used as camel fodder, or reduced to charcoal for the fire ... the crown of an old tree was eaten as a vegetable; the trunk was often tapped for its sugary sap, which could be fermented to make palm toddy.

Food in History (1973)

DURIAN

Diane Armstrong
The Thais consider the durian to be both a delicacy and an aphrodisiac, so we bought one ... opened it at the appropriate moment, cut into it with great curiosity ... and threw it out with even greater haste. Its pervasive, putrid smell lingered in our room for days and we felt we had discovered a cheap weapon in the war against the population explosion.

'Bangkok's Floating Markets', *The Australian* (1977)

John Goode
The durian's taste is sublime
Like strawberries and cream every time,
But its stench is so strong
That to counter the pong
You need peg-on-the-nose when you try 'em.

'The Fruit Bowl of Asia', *Vogue Living* (1982)

Norman Myers ... the experience of consuming a durian can be described as eating an almond-flavoured custard in a public lavatory.

'Tomorrow's menu: chicken with two veg (yahob and wax gourd)', *The Guardian* (c. 1982)

EGGPLANT

Andre Launay The English name of Egg Plant comes from the fact that a rarer of its species is white and looks exactly like a hen's egg. The most common aubergine, however, is long and purple and about the size and as subtle as a handy cosh.

Caviare and After (1964)

Claudia Roden Often called 'poor man's meat' and, in one form, 'poor man's caviar', the aubergine is one of the staple foods of the Middle East ... pick the smaller ones for stuffing. The larger ones can be sliced or cubed and deep-fried, sautéed or stewed.

Middle Eastern Food (1968)

FIGS

John Ray
1628-1705
Peel a fig for your friend,
a peach for your enemy.
English Proverbs

Reay Tannahill In Egypt, whole baskets of figs have been found among the tomb offerings ... The fig, with its mild laxative properties, must have appealed to them as a food which was not only delicious but good for them too.

Food In History (1973)

Andrew Boorde [Figs] doth stere a man to veneryous actes, for they doth urge and increase the sede of generacyon. And also doth provoke a man to sweate; wherefore they doth engender lyce.

A Dyetary of Helth (1542?)

FLOWERS, EDIBLE

John Goode
Some varieties of flowers are suitable for crystallising ... Others may be poisonous including all those grown from bulbs. If sprays are used, only the flowers should be eaten ... Flowers which may be crystallised include: apple blossoms, boronia, cherry blossoms, heather, pear and plum blossoms, primroses and primula including polyanthus, roses, violets.

World Guide to Cooking With Fruit and Vegetables (1973)

FRUIT

Andrew Marvell
1621-78
Ripe Apples drop about my head,
The Luscious Clusters of the Vine
Upon my mouth do crush their Wine;
The Nectaren, and curious Peach,
Into my hands themselves do reach;
Stumbling on Melons, as I pass ...

The Garden

**Sir Arthur
Pinero**
1855-1934
I love fruit, when it is expensive.

The Second Mrs Tanqueray

**'Percy the Poet'
[P. F. Collins]**
Sure, fruit is good at any time,
'Twill make one strong and healthy,
The King, the Queen, the soldier brave,
The poor, likewise the wealthy.
There's Peaches, Pears, and Passion-fruit:
When next you meet Susanna —
Don't be shy, wink your left eye,
And give her a Banana.

'The Power of a Banana', cited by Bill Wannan in
Robust, Ribald and Rude Verse in Australia (1972)

Frank Muir
Fresh fruit was looked upon as dangerous, and until the eighteenth century, the English ate their fruit in dried form: figs, dates and 'raisins of the sun'.

The Frank Muir Book (1978)

GRAPES

Edward FitzGerald
1809-83

Ah, with the Grape my fading Life provide,
And wash my Body whence the life has died.
And in my Windingsheet of Vineleaf wrapt,
So bury me by some sweet Gardenside.
Rubai'yat of Omar Khayyam

Tennyson
1809-92

The foaming grape of eastern France.
In Memorim

Mae West
1892-1980

Beulah, peel me a grape.
I'm No Angel

LAVERBREAD

Sian Llewellyn

Laverbread is a smooth, fine seaweed found off the shores of South Wales. It is gathered daily in ... Penclawdd ... [then] thoroughly washed, to remove all sand and grit ... boiled for 5-6 hours until it is quite soft. The liquid is drained off. This prepared laverbread is sold ... in markets. It should be used and eaten as quickly as possible.
Customs and Cooking from Wales (1974)

Note: In one recipe, cakes of laverbread are coated with oatmeal, and fried in bacon fat for 5-10 minutes. They are served topped with slices of gammon and a fried egg. *J.G.*

LEEKS

Pliny the Elder
c.23-79

Nero ate leeks in oil to improve his voice.
Historia Naturalis

Sian Llewellyn

The leek is one of the national emblems of Wales ... associated with Saint David, who was reputed to have fed upon the leeks that he gathered in the fields ... In A.D. 633, Welshmen wore leeks when fighting Saxon invaders ... Nowadays the leek is worn on Saint David's Day and sported by Welshmen at International Rugby matches.
Customs and Cooking from Wales (1974)

LETTUCE

Mauduit   'Rabbit food', as some English people scornfully call lettuce, can be made delicious, not only as a salad, but as a légume.
The Vicomte in the Kitchen (1933)

Martial
43-104   First there will be given lettuce, useful for relaxing the bowels.
Epigrams

Yann Lovelock   In the Far East, we find lettuce first mentioned in China between A.D. 600 and 900.
The Vegetable Book (1972)

Alexis Soyer   The lettuce — favourite plant of the beautiful Adonis — possesses a narcotic virtue.
Citing Theophrastus and Galen, in *Pantropheon* (1853)

MANGOES

Richard Tipping
1949-   ... Mangoes are fleshy skinful passionate fruits
Mangoes are hungry to be sucked
Mangoes are glad to be stuck in the teeth
Mangoes like slush and kissing.
Mangoes

MANGOSTEEN

John Goode   Malaysian fruit ... resembles an apple [but is] brownish-purple. Flesh has consistency of a greengage and a flavour suggesting ... pineapple, apricot and orange. A delicate fruit, which must be picked ripe and eaten soon after ...
The World Guide to Cooking with Fruit and Vegetables (1973)

Leslie Johns and
Violet Stevenson   ... is used in Indonesia to make vinegar, which indicates it can first be made into wine.
The Complete Book of Fruit (1979)

Anonymous   Some say the King of Thai fruit. Thick pulpy shell with whitish pink meat that melts in your mouth.
Fruits of Thailand (1982)

MELONS

Anonymous   Friends are not all that nifty,
They're much like melons in a shop.
You have to try at least fifty
Before you find one that's tip-top.
Cited in *Feasts of a Militant Gastronome* (1973)

Dorris McFerran Townsend   Ripe and juicy and honey-sweet, melons somehow call up memories of hot, still August weather. Days when even the bees seemed to fly more slowly, and cicadas set up a ceaseless droning. Days when small boys sneaked away from chores with fish poles over their shoulders and the dog for company . . . Days when grandpa thumped his way around the watermelon patch, listening for just the right sound (a dull thud — if the sound was metallic, the melon wasn't yet ripe) . . .
The Cook's Companion (1978)

MULBERRIES

Elizabeth David   If you have just a few mulberries, not enough to make a pudding or an ice, arrange them in a little pyramid, if possible on shiny green leaves, on a plain glass compote dish, with a separate bowl of sugar. They are glorious. But beware the juice. It stains.
Petit Propos Culinaires (1979)

MUSHROOMS

Countess Morphy   . . . the mushroom well deserves to rank as the precious 'pearl of cookery'.
Mushroom Recipes (1954)

Reay Tannahill   Miniature india-rubber mushrooms with nothing
                       to recommend them but their looks.
                       Food in History (1973)

NECTARINE

John Keats   Talking of Pleasure, this moment I was writing
1795-1821   with one hand, and with the other holding to my
                       Mouth a Nectarine — good god, how fine. It went
                       down soft, pulpy, slushy, oozy — all its delicious
                       embonpoint melted down my throat like a large
                       beatified Strawberry. I shall certainly breed.
                       To Charles Dilke, in *Letters*

OLIVES

Walter James   Olives are left on trees to ripen until a dark red or
                       purple colour . . . the fruit — skin, pips and all —
                       is crushed into a pomace . . . then wrapped in
                       cloth and put in a press . . . The mixture of oil and
                       the dark water juice (called blackwater) goes to a
                       tank, where the oil slowly floats to the top and is
                       skimmed off, then filtered and bottled . . .
                       . . . when buying oil, tip the bottle upside
                       down; the longer the oil takes to run back down
                       the neck when the bottle is righted, the purer it
                       will be. (A lot of the 'olive oil' imported into Aus-
                       tralia is half peanut oil . . .)
                       Antipasto (1957)

Tom Stobart   When I lived on the Ligurian coast of Italy . . . we
                       used to head for certain villages in the mountains
                       which had a reputation for producing the finest
                       oil . . . Olive oil was not judged by tasting, but a
                       small quantity was put on the palm . . . the hands
                       rubbed briskly together and . . . the aroma sniffed
                       . . . we all have personal preferences. Some of the
                       oils are light and have a delicate perfume, whilst
                       others are heavy and fruity . . . in mayonnaise, the
                       fruity oils are always inclined to be too powerful
                       . . . it is traditional to use it for cooking and frying,
                       either alone or mixed with lard or butter.
                       Herbs, Spices and Flavourings (1977)

ONIONS

Yann Lovelock   Part of the fun in Anglo-Saxon riddles is to describe one thing in terms of another . . .

> I am a wonderful thing, a joy to women,
> To neighbours useful. I injure no-one,
> No village dweller, save only my slayer.
> I stand up high and steep over the bed;
> Beneath I'm shaggy. Sometimes comes nigh
> A young and handsome peasant's daughter,
> A maiden proud, to lay hold on me,
> She raises my redness, plunders my head,
> Fixes on me fast, feels straightway
> What meeting me means when she thus
>   approaches,
> A curly-haired woman. Wet is that eye.

. . . the above may represent either an onion or a leek . . . since it is often connected with love and lechery.

The Vegetable Book (1972)

Andrew Boorde   Onions do promote a man to veneryous actes, and to somnolence.

A Dyetary of Helthe (1542?)

Upendra Dash,   We don't use onions or garlic . . . because they
(Hare Krishna   arouse the passions.
missionary)   Comment to Australian newspaper, 1970

Anonymous   If leekes you like but do their smell disleek
Eate onyons and you shalle not smelle the leeke.
If you of onyons would the scent expelle,
Eate garlicks, that shalle drowne the onyon's
   smelle.

16th century proverb

Jean Campbell   Loved by the peasant,
Too good for a king,
Better than pheasant,
In fact anything,

Blest dish of onions,
Known as Mare's Nest,

Easing both bunions
And colds on the chest.

'Mare's Nest', cited by Mendelsohn in *A Salute to Onions* (1966)

May Irwin
An onion can make people cry, but has there never been a vegetable invented to make them laugh?

(Attrib.) *Saturday Evening Post* (1931)

Oscar Mendelsohn
Breathes there a man with nose so dead
Who never to himself has said:
'One pickled onion, one shallot,
Would raise this dish to what it's not'?

'Pickled Onions', in *A Salute to Onions* (1966)

PEACHES

Pliny the Elder
c.23-79
As touching peaches in general, the very name in Latin ... *Persica*, doth evidently show that they were brought out of Persia first.

Historia Naturalis

Victor Hugo
1802-85
Its charms richly pleased one's sight
And everyone knew its taste was right
Such skin, as to be beyond one's reach
Like rose and lily joined in bliss
It might have been proud Philis
If, indeed, it hadn't been a peach

Cited in *Feasts of a Militant Gastronome* (1973)

PEAS, GREEN

Charpentier
Are the peas fresh that are offered? ... if a finger-nail is dug into the pod, if sap appears in the wound, the peas are fresh enough.

Those Rich and Great Ones (1935)

Anonymous
I eat my peas with honey,
I've done it all my life.
It makes the peas taste funny
But it keeps 'em on the knife!

Manners

PICKLES AND PICKLING

William
Shakespeare
1564-1616

Stew'd in brine, Smarting in lingering pickle.
Antony and Cleopatra

Alison Burt

A pickle is one or more types of vegetable or fruit preserved in spiced vinegar. [It] keeps its shape and is recognisable in the finished preserve.
Preserves and Pickles (1973)

POMEGRANATES

Walter James

Surely of all dull fruits [the pomegranate] must be the dullest, and surely the drink made from it — grenadine — must be the most syrupy and flavourless.
Antipasto (1957)

Cohier de
Lompier

There are no beautiful dessert fruit baskets without pomegranates ... [one] which has been cut open, looking like a rich treasure of rubies or sparkling garnets, is one of the most beautiful jewels ... aside from this splendid role in the decoration ... [it] does not match the currant in quality. It is not worth any more than the barberry and ... is practically worthless in temperate countries where the 'four red fruits' are abundant and at their best.
Cited in *Dumas on Food* (1978)

POTATOES

Mauduit

It is a gastronomic sin to boil or steam potatoes without their skins ... The difference is patent, you will admit, after tasting of both.
The Vicomte in the Kitchen (1933)

Walter James

... we call a spud after ... a three-pronged fork used in raising the crop.
Antipasto (1957)

Francis Bacon 1561-1626	The best way to cook potatoes is to boil them in beer. *Essays*
[¿] Beauvilliers	France is not the homeland of the potato; the best ones come from Holland. *L'Art du cuisinier* (mid-19th century)
Jerome K. Jerome 1859-1927	Harris and I started to peel the potatoes. I should never have thought that peeling potatoes was such an undertaking ... We began cheerfully ... but our lightheartedness was gone by the time the first potato was finished. The more we peeled, the more peel there seemed to be left on ... George came and had a look at it — it was about the size of a peanut. He said 'Oh, that won't do! You're wasting them. You must scrape them.' *Three Men in a Boat*
Viherjuuri, M., Tanttu, A-M. and J.	The first *new potatoes*, in June: always a wonderful experience to the Finns. These tiny, finger-tip-sized, boiled new potatoes, dill from your own patch, and fresh butter. You don't need anything else. *Finlandia Gastronomica* (1974)
'Bon Viveur', [John and Fanny Cradock]	'Mashed potatoes' are certainly family fodder. Even so ... it is no great chore to transform the mixture from a rather gloomy, forked-up, grey-white hump which looks like a Saxon burial ground into *pommes duchesse* or good, golden *pommes croquettes*. *Daily Telegraph Sociable Cook Book* (1967)
Rudolph Nureyev 1938-	Only potatoes mattered to me — they were worth their weight in gold, let alone their weight in prayers ... The mornings [of his childhood] began ... with goat cheese and potatoes. *Autobiography*

RHUBARB

Ambrose Bierce 1842-c.1914	Rhubarb: vegetable essence of stomach ache. *The Enlarged Devil's Dictionary*

SEAWEED

Prosper Montagné

It is said that the inhabitants of Iceland, the Faroe Islands, Scotland, Norway, Denmark and North America use it as food. It is, however, only eaten in times of scarcity, except in Scotland, where the young stems of sea-lettuce are sometimes eaten as a salad. This dish ... has not found much favour with any visitors who have tasted it. Matters are quite different ... in Japan ... *Amanori* and *kombu* ... are greatly prized for their gelatinous properties, though ... these products are used more as condiments ...

'Sea Wrack, Rock Weed', *Larousse Gastronomique* (1972)

Shizuo Tsuji

Since the flavour and nutrients of giant kelp [*kombu*] pass quickly into clear water ... a lengthy soaking, 8 hours or overnight, yields a delicious and subtle liquid ... used in primary *dashi* in lieu of heating the kelp in water ... with the addition of the dried bonito flakes.

'Kelp Stock', *Japanese Cooking, A Simple Art* (1980)

'Cassandra' [William Connor]

I have gathered it from the rocks on the shores of County Derry, where it is known as dulse ... You can eat it raw, or boil it and serve with whelks or haddocks. You can even roast it on tongs. I have no hesitation in saying that this slimy meal is the most revolting mess I have ever tasted.

'The Green, Green Grass of Home', *Daily Mirror* (1964)

SPINACH

Walter James

Add nutmeg to spinach.
Antipasto (1957)

Wilma Pezzini

... in terms of international gastronomy, to say 'florentine' is to say 'spinach'. Actually, spinach made this way is eaten all over Tuscany.
The Tuscan Cookbook (1979)

Yann Lovelock   The Arabs thought highly of it, naming it 'the prince of vegetables' ... in the U.S. during the 1920s, it was ... pushed commercially ... one of the selling points being its truly remarkable effect in the adventures of Popeye the Sailorman.

The Vegetable Book (1972)

STRAWBERRIES

R. W. Emerson   Strawberries lose their flavour in garden beds.
1803-82   'Prudence' *Essays, First Series*

Anonymous   But sit on a cushion
And sew a fine seam
And feed upon strawberries
Sugar and cream.
Curly Locks

Izaak Walton   ... as Dr Boteler said of strawberries: 'Doubtless
1593-1683   God would have made a better berry, but doubt-less God never did'.
The Compleat Angler

SWEET POTATO

Owen Wister   Said Aristotle unto Plato,
1860-1938   'Have another sweet potato?'
Said Plato unto Aristotle,
'Thank you, I prefer the bottle.'
Philosophy

TOMATOES

Diana Kennedy   Mexican tomatoes must be among the best in the world ... what a joy it is for city dwellers to suddenly find them [fat, juicy and sweet] ... instead of the low quality tasteless ones usually available ... of all the cuisines that rely heavily on tomatoes ... they were only introduced into Spain in the 16th century ... [by some] at that time they were considered to be unhealthy and by others an aphrodisiac, therefore forbidden to women.

The Cuisines of Mexico (1972)

TOMATO JUICE

Anonymous

An accident happened to my brother Jim
When somebody threw a tomato at him —
Tomatoes are juicy and don't hurt the skin,
But this one was specially packed in a tin.

'Ware tomato-juice', cited in *Verse and Worse* (1952)

TRUFFLES

Robert Darroch

Scientists discovered that the appeal of the truffle is not so much its exoticism as its eroticism . . . it contains the hormone androstenol . . . Three German scientists [have] shown that if a group of men and women are exposed to a spray of dilute androstenol they, too, become sexually aroused.

'The Mystery of Truffles Solved', *Bulletin* (1982)

Robert Courtine

Lamazère is a kind of truffle trainer . . . one always has the feeling that truffles are miraculous illusory creatures. Lamazère arrives with empty hands . . . and presto! a black diamond sparkles in his palm: a fat truffle . . . It is therefore unimaginable that this magician would be stingy enough to scrape the fat truffle like a hazelnut to make it last a week, or carve the diamond into tiny chips to set in junk jewellery! No! Lamazère serves you the whole truffle with salt, as is proper . . . One cuts off a slice, butters it, salts it, crunches it! Curses on anyone who is not piggish enough . . . to swallow a whole basket of them served that way.

'Roger Lamazère', *Feasts of a Militant Gastronome* (1973)

**Ann Barr and
Bill Levy**

. . . the black or périgord tuber *Melanosporum*, and the white tuber *Magnata* are the most precious substances . . . the strongly-perfumed black truffle can be cooked whole, but is usually used in tiny slivers to flavour other food. In the great truffle shortage, people joked that Foodies were adding shavings of rubber tyres to the truffles. Even the more strongly-scented white truffle is never cooked, but shaved over your risotto with a razor device to keep the slices paper-thin . . . the fungus really hit the fan in November 1982 when two journalists from Britain (Jane Grigson and Paul Levy) discovered that even the *white* truffle could be cultivated.

'The Great Truffle Scandal', *The Official Foodie Handbook* (1985)

Alexandre Dumas
1802-70

I put them in a class apart, for they do not lend themselves to promiscuity . . . not so much as a mushroom, or as a rare and exquisite food, but as a work of art: it is the ambrosia of the gods, the *sacrum sacrorum* of gastronomes.

Grand Dictionnaire de Cuisine

Brillat-Savarin
1755-1826

Whosoever pronounces the word *truffle* . . . awakens erotic and gastronomical dreams equally in the sex that wears skirts and the one that sprouts a beard . . . the diamond in the art of cookery . . . the truffle contributes to the sexual pleasures . . . The truffle is not a positive aphrodisiac, but it can in certain situations, make women tenderer and men more agreeable.

Physiologie du Goût

W. M. Thackeray
1811-63

Presently we were aware of an odour gradually coming towards us, something musky, fiery, savoury, mysterious — a hot, drowsy smell, that lulls the senses and yet enflames them — the truffles were coming.

Memorials of Gourmandising

Colette
1873-1954

'Most capricious and revered of black princesses'.

Cited by Glynn Christian in *Delicatessen Food Handbook* (1983)

Andre Launay

. . . its one redeeming feature is its unique and remarkable aroma. Place a truffle on a dozen new laid eggs and 24 hours later all the eggs will taste of truffle.

Caviare and After (1964)

TURNIPS

John Updike
1932-

She took the turnpike
And travelled to Dover,
Where turnips enjoy
A rapid turnover.

'Upon Hearing that a Bird Exists Called the Turnstone'

Samuel Johnson
1709-84

If the man who turnips cries,
Cry not when his father dies,
'Tis a proof that he had rather
Have a turnip than his father!

His riposte to a London street cry, in *Old London Street Cries* by Andrew W. Tuer (1885)

VEGETABLES

Charpentier

... it is a deception and ... improper when vegetables and salad greens are displayed dripping wet. Poor plants revive in their bath, but they have ceased to be fresh garden produce ... Such things should never be placed in water ... what is gained to the eye is lost to the palate ... parsley will absorb water like a sponge but it will lose its aroma. All green things lose some of their flavour when they are rejuvenated with water.

Those Rich and Great Ones (1935)

Elizabeth David

Florentine cooks ... who followed later with Marie de Medici were responsible for the introduction into France of new vegetables (artichokes, haricot beans, broccoli, savoy cabbages, *petits pois*) and new methods of cultivation.

Italian Food (1979)

Beau Brummell
1778-1840

I once ate a pea!

Reply to being asked if he ate vegetables

Eliza Acton

Vegetables when not sufficiently cooked are known to be exceedingly unwholesome and indigestible, that the custom of serving them *crisp*, which means, in reality, only half-boiled, should be altogether disregarded ... when health is considered more important than fashion ...

Modern Cooking for Private Families (1845)

MEAT, FOWL AND FISH

ALLIGATOR

A. Hyatt Verrill   The tail of a young alligator is clear, white, flaky and delicate, so similar to fillet of flounder . . . that few persons distinguish one from the other.
Foods America Gave the World (n.d.)

Marjorie Rawlings   . . . alligator — like liver or veal . . . had to be cooked very quickly or else for a very long time, because between, it toughened . . .
Cross Creek Cookery (1942)

ARBROATH SMOKIES

David Mabey   . . . small haddock, beheaded but kept whole, and hot smoked so that the flesh is cooked and the skin outside is copper . . . one of the rarer types of smoked fish, and certainly one of the most delicious.
In Search of Food (1978)

ARMADILLO

Faith Medlin   An Armadillo Festival is held in Victoria, Texas every Memorial Day weekend; citizens compete for honors . . . as well as in cooking them. The tender white flesh of this pork-flavored animal is praised by those who know, especially when barbecued. It was sometimes called 'Hoover-hog' or 'poor-man's pig' in Texas during the Great Depression.
A Gourmet's Book of Beasts (1975)

BEEF

Ogden Nash
1902-71

Just purloin a sirloin, my pet,
If you'd win a devotion incredible . . .
The Clean Platter

Henry Fielding
1707-54

When mighty roast beef was the Englishman's
     food
It enobled our hearts and enriched our blood —
Our soldiers were brave and our courtiers were
     good.
Oh! The roast beef of England,
Old England's roast beef.
Grub Street Opera

**Charles II,
King of England**
(1630-85)

For its merit, I will knight it and make it
Sir-Loin!
     On being told that a piece of beef that particularly
     pleased him was called the loin.

Anonymous

Fillet steak is very nice
Rump is too, but, oh the price!
     So let's cook mince,
     And price won't pinch.
     Cited in *Talking About Tucker* (1975)

Mark Twain
1835-1910

. . . beefsteak. They have it in Europe, but they
don't know how to cook it. Neither will they cut
it right. It lies in the centre of [a small, round
pewter platter] a bordering bed of grease-soaked
potatoes; it is the size, shape and thickness of a
man's hand with the thumb and fingers cut off. It
is a little overdone, is rather dry, it tastes pretty
insipidly, it rouses no enthusiasm.
     'European Diet', *A Tramp Abroad*

**Katherine
Mansfield**
1885-1923

England is merely an island of beef flesh swimming in a warm gulf stream of gravy.
The Modern Soul

BOMBAY DUCK

Faith Medlin

. . . not a duck at all but a phosphorescent fish, the
Bunmallow [bummalo] from the estuaries of
northern India. It is dried and tinned in Bombay.

The flavour . . . is quite transformed when toasted over a flame. It can be munched as an hors d'oeuvre or crumbled into a curry.

A Gourmet's Book of Beasts (1975)

Carol Willson and John Goode

. . . similar fish are also salted and dried in Indonesia and other parts of South-East Asia . . . Because of its very strong smell and taste . . . always used as an accompaniment, mostly with rice, but also with other sambals.

The Original Australian and New Zealand Fish Cookbook (1981)

BONE

Anonymous

Fee, fie, fo, fum,
I smell the blood of an Englishman;
Be he alive or be he dead,
I'll grind his bones to make my bread.

Nursery rhyme

CAPON

Gabriel Vicaire

Suddenly we saw — gay, fresh and hale
As a smiling new wife —
A capon from the banks of the Veyle
That had bloomed with new life . . .
It was so unctuous to behold,
The cook gave the impression
Of someone who marches
In a religious procession.

Cited by Courtine in *Feasts of a Militant Gastronome* (1973)

CAVIARE

J. C. Edmonds

Beluga . . . colour ranges from grey-white to dark grey, but is rarely black . . . Sevruga is slightly darker . . . but is of exceptional quality . . . Least common is the Volga sturgeon which produces the legendary golden caviar of the tsars

[Ocietrova] ... Red caviar is the trade name for salmon caviar ... the larger glistening roe of Pacific salmon ... Whitefish roe from North America and lumpfish roe from the Arctic Sea are probably better known. [They] only get their jet black and lipstick red colouring when processed in vegetable dye.

'You Pay the World for Caviar ... ' *Sydney Morning Herald* (c.1980)

Andre Launay

Caviare is a delicate seafood, so delicate it should be eaten solely as a unique experience and not drowned with wine or pints of vodka as is customary in all good Hollywood versions of life under the Tsars ... an ounce of caviare rolled in smoked salmon will produce mumbles of ecstasy.

Caviare and After (1964)

Note: In his introduction, Launay suggests the only real way to enjoy caviare is on a spoon, by the spoonful. The one occasion on which this was possible was at the Imperial Hotel, Tokyo, in October 1981 when, at a function and buffet, a huge mound of Sevruga on a bed of ice lay untouched, and the general manager encouraged us to really enjoy it. We did and it was divine! *J.G.*

Ann Bridge

Every morning, in Moscow [in the spring of 1941] there appeared upon my breakfast-tray a huge rack of perfect toast, a great lump of yellow butter, and a large glass sugar-bowl containing about half a pound [250g] of caviare — the fresh, grey, translucent, softly-tinted pearls of pleasure ... try it with well-made coffee, alone and in bed, with the question of quantity wholly absent! It is a wonderful experience.

'Food in Three Continents' (c.1943)

Anonymous

He: 'Tell me, my dear, how did you find the caviar?'
She: 'Oh, quite by accident, when I lifted the quail egg.'

Caption from a cartoon in a French publication, cited in *Feasts of a Militant Gastronome* (1973)

CHICKEN

Henry IV of France
I want there to be no peasant in my kingdom so poor that he is unable to have a chicken in his pot every Sunday.
> Cited by Hardouin de Perefixe, *Histoire de Henry le Grand* (1681)

Robert Courtine
I won't mention the name of the place in which I was brought a fowl to carve whose flesh I couldn't cut (I swear), not even with carving scissors and a hammer.
> *Feasts of a Militant Gastronome* (1973)

Peter Porter
1929-
London is full of chickens on electric spits
Cooking in windows where the public pass.
This, say the chickens, is their Auschwitz,
And all poultry-eaters are psychopaths.
> 'Annotations of Auschwitz'

CORNED BEEF

Jean Hewitt
Corned beef has nothing to do with corn [maize], but got the name from 'corns', or grains, of saltpetre or gunpowder used in curing.
> *New England Heritage Cookbook* (1979)

COW

E. M. Root
1895-¿
God's jolly cafeteria
With four legs and a tail.
> *The Cow*

R. L. Stevenson
1850-94
The friendly cow, all red and white,
I love with all my heart,
She gives me cream with all her might,
To eat with apple tart.
> *The Cow*

CRAB

William Shakespeare
1564-1616

And Marian's nose looks red and raw,
When roasted crabs hiss in the bowl.
Love's Labour's Lost

G. W. Cable and L. Hearn

. . . those delightfully innocent, tender creatures, soft-shell crabs.
Historical Sketchbook and Guide to New Orleans (1885)

CROCODILE

Alexander Lake

The musk glands of the neck are offensive and must first be removed. 'Broil thin slices of crocodile, add sweet red wine, ginger and salt to the resulting sauce, pour liquid over the meat, with grated cheese and butter, bake in a fast oven until browned and serve with sautéed sliced mushrooms.
Hunter's Choice (n.d.)

L. M. D'Albertis
1841-1901

I took it into my head to play a trick on Wilcox and Bob . . . The Chinese cook and I roasted the crocodile and boiled the turtle. When dinner time came, Wilcox and Bob both found the roast meat much better than the boiled . . . when they discovered what it was, they were very near pitching the plates and forks into the river . . . I had some qualms afterwards but I reflected that even had the father and mother of this crocodile been guilty of eating human flesh, he himself, at his tender age, must certainly be innocent of such an act.
New Guinea: What I Did, What I Saw (1880)

CRUSTACEA

Sandy Watson

He may, if he so chooses to,
Beneath the unction of the lawn
Unveil the feelers of the prawn,
Or, from the lobster pots of sin
Extract a pensive Paladin.
'Under Currents' (n.d.)

Anonymous

Be lenient with lobsters, and ever kind to crabs,
And be not disrespectful to cuttle fish or dabs . . .

'Lines by a Humanitarian'

Robert Brough
1828-60

I'm a shrimp, I'm a shrimp of diminutive size.
Inspect my antennae, and look at my eyes;
I'm a natural syphon, when dipped in a cup,
For I drain the contents to the last drop up.
I care not for crawfish, I heed not the prawn,
From a flavour especial my fame has been drawn;
Nor e'en the crab or the lobster do yield,
When I'm properly cooked and efficiently peeled.
Quick! Quick! pile the coals — let your saucepan
be deep,
For the weather is warm, and I'm sure not to
keep;
Off, off with my head — split my shell into
three —
I'm a shrimp! I'm a shrimp! — to be eaten with
tea.

'I'm a Shrimp! I'm a Shrimp!'

DUCK

Martial
43-104

Let a duck certainly be served up whole; but it is
tasty only in the breast and neck: the rest return to
the cook.

Epigrams

EELS

Eliza Acton

Eels should be alive and brisk in movement when
they are purchased, but the 'horrible barbarity', as
it is truly designated, of skinning and dividing
them while they are so, is without excuse, as they
are easily destroyed 'by piercing the spinal
marrow close to the back part of the skull with a
sharp-pointed knife or skewer.'

Modern Cookery (1845)

Anonymous

Large silver eels — a groat a pound, live eels!
Not the Severn's famed stream
Could produce better fish,
Sweet and fresh as new cream,
And what more could you wish.

Old London Street Cries (1885)

John Goode and Carol Willson

. . . few people could have matched our first experience at catching eels. These were on the upper reaches of a river in northern New South Wales. They were located with spotlights, and shot with a .22 rifle at 2 a.m. As we had to bag the stunned catch, this was quite a job, as eels have sharp teeth.

The Original Australia and New Zealand Fish Cookbook (1979)

EGGS

OBSERVATION

Charles A. Dana
1819-97

All the goodness of a good egg cannot make up for the badness of a bad one.

The Making of a Newspaper Man

Anonymous

'I'm afraid you've got a bad egg, Mr Jones!'
'Oh no, my Lord, I assure you! Parts of it are excellent!'

'The Curate's Egg', *Punch* (1895)

Roy Bishop
1895-?

The egg is smooth and very pale;
It has no nose, it has no tail;
It has no ears that one can see;
It has no wit, no repartee.

The Inefficacious Egg

Samuel Butler
1835-1902

The hen is only an egg's way of making another egg.

Life and Habit

Rudyard Kipling
1865-1936

Being kissed by a man who didn't wax his moustache was — like eating an egg without salt.

'Poor Dear Mamma', *The Story of the Gadsbys*

Oliver Herford
1863-1935

Alas! My child, where is the Pen,
That can do justice to the hen?
. . . Laying foundations every day,
Though not for Public Buildings, yet
For Custard, Cakes and Omelette.
. . . No wonder, Child, we prize the Hen,
Whose egg is mightier than the Pen.

The Hen

PREPARATION

**M. F. K. Fisher
(trans.)**

'a perfectly boiled egg' . . . is unsullied, and pure in
form. It is a challenge to any human being's sense
of balance, of time, and of taste. It has submitted
to none of man's gastronomical caprices.

Physiology of Taste

Jane Austen
1775-1817

'An egg boiled very soft is not unwholesome,'
said Mr Woodhouse.

Emma

Gertrude Stein
1874-1946

Helene [her Parisian cook] said, after being told
that Matisse would be staying to dinner: 'In that
case I will not make an omelette, but fry the eggs
. . . it shows less respect and he will understand!'

Autobiography of Alice B. Toklas

William King

I am much of his [Horace's] opinion, and could
only wish that the world was thoroughly informed of two other truths concerning eggs —
one is how incomparably better roasted eggs are
than boiled; the other — never to eat any butter
with an egg in the shell.

Cited by Leyel and Hartley in *The Gentle Art of
Cookery* (1925)

H. A. Field

At breakfast, if her egg were fried,
'Oh bring me boiled or poached,' she cried,
But boiled or poached, as you may guess,
Would satisfy her even less . . .

The Food Fad (n.d.)

**Thomas
Hamilton**

One nasty custom . . . Eggs, instead of being eaten
from the shell, are poured into a wine glass and,
after being duly and disgustingly churned up with

butter and condiment, the mixture . . . is forth-
with either spooned into the mouth, or drunk off
like liquid.

Men and Manners in America (n.d.)

RARA OVA

Mauduit

Penguin eggs: greenish white . . . about the size of
a turkey's, should be eaten hard-boiled, cold with
a salad. To hard-boil them takes about three-
quarters of an hour; when shelled, the whites appear like pale green jelly . . . they are delicious to
the taste as they are attractive to the eye.

The Vicomte in the Kitchen (1933)

Anonymous

Teach not thy parent's mother to extract
The embryo juices of the bird by suction.
The good old lady can that feat enact
Quite irrespective of thy kind instruction.

'Cuckoo effect'

ELEPHANT

**Laurens van der
Post**

Europeans . . . created what I call 'curiosity cooking' . . . It was said that District Commissioners,
out in the bush, always ate a dish of elephant
head and trotters on Sundays. I have seen my
own bearers go wild with excitement [and they]
would eat elephant as if it were caviare — largely
perhaps because their traditional diet is deprived
of meat . . . I have often tried elephant and I find it
edible . . . the equivalent in the bush of whale
meat at sea . . . too giant a texture ever to be truly
palatable. A great favourite of the 'curiosity cook'
has always been the tip of the tongue and the
pads and lower joint of the foot.

First Catch Your Eland (1977)

Sir Samuel Baker

The natives of Ceylon [Sri Lanka] refuse the flesh
of the elephant as do mostly those of India. I have
frequently eaten it in Africa . . . and although inferior to beef or mutton, I have considered it too
good to waste. The fat, when boiled down, is

useful for cooking purposes, or for making soap, and the foot is excellent if baked ... in a slow oven ... The result will not be satisfactory under thirty-six hours ...

True Tales for My Grandson (1884)

Alexis Soyer The Romans never evinced fondness for the flesh of the elephant. We cannot, however, affirm that the gastronomic eccentricity of some Roman epicure did not dream of a monstrous feast, in which he may have offered to his guests an elephant *a la Troyenne* on a silver dish, made purposely for the occasion.

The Pantropheon (1853)

FISH

John Goode and Carol Willson Local prejudices, based on supply, may also be influential. At Normanton in north-west Queensland, estuarial catfish are knocked on the head and thrown back to feed crocodiles and sharks ... However, at Cairns, 800 km to the east, local anglers ... consider they make an excellent meal.

The Original Australia and New Zealand Fish Cookbook (1979)

Mauduit ... fish should always be eaten out of the sea ... except turbot, which improves after being under running water for a few hours ... shellfish should never be cooked except on the day they have been taken ... or at the most, on the following day. The shellfish, though he remains alive after being taken from the water, has a known habit of brooding when out of his element ... and we must look out for the effects on ourselves of his melancholy, which results in creating a poison which is not got rid of by cooking ... Never buy a cooked lobster ... unless you have seen it when alive. Always cook your own crabs; never buy cooked shrimps.

The Vicomte in the Kitchen (1933)

Jonathan Swift
1667-1745

Fish should swim thrice: first it should swim in the sea ... then it should swim in butter, and at last, sirrah, it should swim in good claret.

Polite Conversation

Walter de la Mare
1873-1956

Ann, Ann!
Come quick as you can!
There's a fish that *talks*
In the frying pan.

'Alas, Alack'

Alexander Pope
1688-1744

'Tis true, no turbots dignify my boards,
But gudgeons, flounders, what my Thames affords.

Imitations of Horace

FISH FINGERS

Marika Hanbury Tenison

... freezing has also given us such horrors as the 'fish finger', so that for many people the word 'fish' is associated with a piece of tasteless blotting-paper, oblong ... with a coating of synthetic orange-coloured crumbs.

The Best of British Cooking (1976)

FROG'S LEGS

Ogden Nash
1902-71

You order legs of frog, and please omit the garlic;
They bring you legs of frog, all redolent of garlic.
Throw the frogs' legs on the floor,
That's what the floor is for.

Try it Suns and Hols; It's Closed Then

GIRAFFE

Laurens van der Post

... [giraffe] marrow is perhaps the oldest and most sought-after delicacy of primitive man in Africa.

First Catch Your Eland (1977)

GOOSE

Jacob Poole
1774-1827

A goose is a silly bird, too much for one, not enough for two.

> Reply to a Walsall man, asked if he would have a goose for the family's Christmas dinner
> *Archaic Words*

Charles Gerard

The bird itself is nothing, but the art of man has turned it into an instrument which produces marvellous results, a kind of living greenhouse in which the supreme fruit of gastronomy is grown.

> *L'Ancienne Alsace à table*

GRASSHOPPERS

Charles V. Riley

... generally prepared by first detaching the legs and wings. The bodies are then either boiled, roasted, stewed, fried or broiled [grilled]. The Romans are said to have ... carefully roasted them to a bright yellow ... [in the 1870s] in most parts of Africa, and especially in Russia, they are salted or smoked like red herrings ... I was ... agreeably surprised to find that the insects were quite palatable, in whatever way prepared. The flavour of the raw locust is most strong and disagreeable, but that of the cooked insect ... is sufficiently mild to be easily neutralised by anything with which they may be mixed ...

> *Proceedings, American Association for the Advancement of Science* (1875)

Note: In Thailand, fried grasshoppers and cicadas were still being sold and eaten in 1984. Like many similar 'snacks', those sampled seemed to be grossly over-rated. However, a bottle of cicada essence (its correct name is only in Thai and indecipherable) is a fantastic last-minute addition to soups and stews. *J.G.*

GROUSE

Edmond de Goncourt
1822-96

... grouse [at Zola's] whose scented flesh Daudet compared to an old courtesan's flesh marinaded in a bidet.

> *Journal*

134

David Mabey

Of all varieties of feathered game, the red grouse ... has the finest and most subtle flavour ... It thrives on the berries and tender young shoots of highland heather ... Alexis Soyer suggested that birds be wrapped in sprigs of heather and moistened with whisky before being roasted ... birds should always be hung for at least three or four days, possibly as long as ten days, depending on the weather ... can be stuffed with fresh rowanberries, cranberries, or even wild raspberries.

In Search of Food (1978)

HAM

Andre Launay

A real York ham is something very different from the pappy, salty, anaemic stuff that is passed off as ham in sandwiches ... Bayonne and Parma hams are served raw ... It is raw, salt meat, extremely delicate in taste and has the peculiarity of, if cooked, becoming quite uneatable, being both tough and too salty.

Caviare and After (1964)

HERRINGS

Günter Grass
1927-

They [herrings] can be used fresh, salted, smoked, or marinated. They can be boiled, baked, fried, steamed, filleted, boned and stuffed, rolled around gherkins, or placed in oil, vinegar, white wine and sour cream. Boiled with onions in salt water they went very well with Amanda Woyke's potatoes in their jackets. Sophie Rotzoll laid them on strips of bacon, sprinkled them with breadcrumbs and popped them into the oven. Margaret Rusch, the cooking nun, liked to steam sauerkraut with juniper berries and throw in small, boned Baltic herrings towards the end. Agnes Kurbiella served tender fillets steamed in white wine as diet fare, Lena Stubbe rolled herrings in flour, fried them, and set them before her second husband.

The Flounder (1978)

HIPPOPOTAMUS

Laurens van der Post The hippopotamus has ... the finest natural lard of any animal ... great hunters assured me that [this] lard was so sweet and tasty that one could eat it raw.

First Catch Your Eland (1977)

HORSEFLESH

Alexander Dumas 1802-70 Horsemeat is ... closer grained than beef ... highly nitrogenised, and consequently very nutritious, it is very doubtful if it could ever become daily fare. M. de Sainte-Hilaire has tried in vain ... through his *agapes* of horse, to get this animal firmly established in Parisian butchers'.

Dumas on Food (1979)

Anonymous *Sakuraniki*: 'cherry blossom meat' (horseflesh).

Japanese guide to food

Prosper Montagné ... an ardent propaganda campaign in favour of horsemeat [in Paris] was crowned by success when, on 6 February 1865, a horsemeat banquet was held at the Grand Hotel ... Since then, horsemeat has become more and more popular.

Larousse Gastronomique (1938)

KANGAROO

Oliver Goldsmith 1728-74 One [Kangaroo] that was killed proved to be good food; but a second, which weighed eighty-four pounds [38kg] was not yet come to its full growth, [and] was found to be much inferior

Citing Sir Joseph Banks and others in 'The Gerbua', *Animated Nature*

Alexandre Dumas 1802-70 The flesh of the kangaroo is excellent, especially when it has grown up wild ... [it] is eminently favourable to the production of good quality meat, greatly preferable to that of the cow or sheep in that it is more tender than the first and

much more abundant and nutritious than the
second.

Dumas on Food, translated by Alan and Jane Davidson
(1978)

Note: This entry of Dumas' is pure fiction. If he had had
to skin a 'roo or wallaby, he would realise the tough-
ness of its attachment and the extreme number of sin-
ews. Except in a drought, the growth rate of a kangaroo
would not compare with that of any domesticated
beast. Medlin, in *A Gourmet's Book of Beasts* (Eriksson,
New York, 1975), perpetrates this by adding 'Kangaroo
meat has been compared to wild rabbit and has also
been described as more tender than beef and more
nourishing than mutton' (p.81). Obviously she had
never cooked or tasted it! What she writes and what no
one stresses is that kangaroo flesh is tough, and needs
prolonged cooking. It conflicts with all the compiler's
personal and first-hand knowledge of cooking kangaroo and wallaby. *J.G.*

KIDNEYS

Ann Bridge ... in the spring of 1941 ... in Moscow ... kidneys could be bought, but very oddly — calves',
sheep's, pigs' and ox-kidneys were all chopped up
together into lumps, and sold in a heterogeneous
and distasteful mass.

'Food in Three Continents' (c.1943)

LAMB AND MUTTON

Thomas Fuller
1654-1734
Of all birds, give me mutton.
Gnomologia

**Oliver
Goldsmith**
1728-74
... to poets who seldom can eat,
Your very good mutton's a very good treat ...
The Haunch of Venison

Andre Simon Excellent lamb is obtainable in England, but it is
practically impossible to get really good mutton
... Haricot mutton is a misnomer: it is a stew
with a *sauce brune*, and no haricot beans what-
soever ... from the old French verb *haligoter*
meaning to cut up in small pieces
The Art of Good Living (1951)

Marika Hanbury Tenison

... lamb was more frequently eaten in the Mediterranean countries, from which we have learned to cook our [British] lamb with rosemary and lemon ... classic British dishes can be truly delicious if they are made of young English lamb ... New Zealand lamb, which is often tender but frequently lacking in flavour, can be improved by marinading and again by the subtle use of herbs and spices.

The Best of British Cooking (1976)

Note: In New Zealand, no one could agree with the above comment. New Zealand lamb has a superb flavour when fresh, unlike Australian lamb, which is virtually flavourless when bought fresh but which can be made delicious by impaling with slivers of garlic and then rubbing the skin with salt and lemon juice. *J.G.*

Gerald Dee

Henry Sutton
Made his wife
Serve him mutton
All his life.

When going to sleep
His mind was rested
By counting the sheep
That he'd digested.

Henry Sutton (n.d.)

Thomas Hood
1799-1845

There are wholesale eaters who can devour a leg of mutton at a sitting.

Review of Arthur Coningsby (1838)

Sydney Smith
1771-1845

Hell is a thousand years of tough mutton.

Cited by Philippa Pullar in *Consuming Passions*

X. M. Boulestin

In Périgord ... I tried to convince my father of the charm of London ... 'and you mean to tell me that they eat mint with lamb?' I assured him that it was delicious. 'What a funny country,' he replied, shaking his head. 'Now a clove of garlic inserted near the bone, yes, but mint ...'

Ease and Endurance (1948)

LAMPREY

Sheila Hutchins   Henry I, the youngest son of William the Conquerer, died of a surfeit of lampreys ... Still popular in France, they are eaten ... all along the river Loire, and in Bordeaux.

Royal Cookbook (1971)

Carol Willson   ... At the market in Helsinki, it is common to see
and John Goode   someone buying a hot-smoked lamprey, about 25cm long, and eating its delicious white flesh as a snack.

'Exciting and Unexpected Finland', *Good Housekeeping* (1984)

LIVER

May Byron   Liver Ketchup: Take a bullock's liver, wash it extremely well, then put it with some salt in four quarts [4.55 litres] of water. Let it simmer away one-half, carefully skimming it all the time. Strain it through a hair sieve, and let it stand till next day, then pour it gently into a saucepan with spice, a clove of garlic, a few bay leaves, and a bit of horse-radish. When boiled enough to season, let it stand till cold and bottle it for use.

Early 19th century Lancashire recipe, in *Pot Luck: The British Home Cookery Book*

LOBSTER AND CRAYFISH

Samuel Butler   And like a lobster boiled, the morn
1835-1902   From black to red began to turn.

Hudibras

Emile Zola   'You would have had very poor fare ... Saffre has
1840-1902   no culinary imagination whatever. His idea of a good meal is a lobster salad'.

La Curée

Elizabeth David   Then there is a recipe for a sauce for lobster which I came across in a French dictionary of cooking of the 1830s. Among the collection of outlandish ingredients were anisette liqueur and soy sauce . . . Why not try it? I did and came to the conclusion that it was the best sauce for lobster ever invented.

'Whisky in the Kitchen', *An Omelette and a Glass of Wine* (1984)

LOCUSTS

William Shakespeare
1564-1616

The food that to him now is as luscious as locusts, shall be to him shortly as bitter as coloquintida [a bitter drug obtained from a type of cucumber].

Othello

New Testament

His meat was locusts and wild honey.

St Matthew

MACKEREL

Josh Billings
1818-85

The mackrel iz a game fish. They ought tew be well edukated, for they are always in schools . . . those which inhabit the grocerys alwus taste to me az tho they had been born and fatted on salt. They want a good deal ov freshning before they are eaten . . . If I can hav plenty ov mackrel for breakfast i can generally make the other two meals out ov cold water.

The Mackrel

Dorothy Hartley

When buying, it should be 'so fresh that the light shines from it like a rainbow'.

Food in England (n.d.)

Jane Grigson

. . . svelte and beautiful fish.

Fish Cookery (1975)

MEAT

Samuel Johnson
1709-84

Any of us would kill a cow rather than not have beef.

Boswell's *Life of Johnson*

Jean Jacques Rousseau
1712-1778

Great eaters of meat are in general more cruel and ferocious than other men. The cruelty of the English is known.

Émile

Lord Byron
1788-1824

But man is a carnivorous production,
And must have meals, at least one meal a day . . .
Although his anatomical construction
Bears vegetables in a grumbling way,
Your labouring people think beyond question
Beef, veal and mutton, better for digestion.

Don Juan

Isaak Walton
1593-1683

This dish of meat is too good for any but anglers, or very honest men.

The Compleat Angler

Katharine Whitehorn

One man's meat is another man's cocktail sausage.

Cooking in a Bedsitter (1963)

Marcel Proust
1871-1922

Since [Francoise] attached the utmost importance to the intrinsic value of the materials . . . she herself would go to the Halles to procure the finest cuts of rump steak, shins of beef, and calves' feet, just as Michelangelo spent eight months in Carrara selecting the most perfect blocks of marble for the monument of Julius II.

Swann's Way

Confucius
c.550-478 B.C.

Meat must be minced finely . . . though there may be a large quantity, one should not exceed the proportion of rice . . . Meat that is not properly cut must not be eaten.

Cited in *Royal Cookbook* (1971)

G. K. Chesterton
1874-1936

He crams with cans of poisoned meat
The subjects of the King,
And when they die by thousands,
Why, he laughs like anything.

'Song against Grocers'

MUSSELS

Mauduit

... when cooking mussels, clams, etc., always add to them a sixpence, for if the sixpence retains its silvery appearance you are absolutely safe. If the sixpence turns black, you are not.

The Vicomte in the Kitchen (1933)

Note: Whether this will apply in the days of cupro-nickel 'silver' coins is not known. Old threepenny and sixpenny bits contained real silver, but the advocacy of this is doubted, because the author claims this will tell if fungi are poisonous or not, which is a false assumption. J.G.

Jane Grigson

... it is sad that mussels are generally regarded, both here and in America, as the poor man's shellfish ... they lack the piquancy of clams, or the exquisite distinction of oysters, but they have a voluptuous sweetness of their own ...

Fish Cookery (1975)

OCTOPUS

C. S. Sonnini

In order to soften the membraneous substance ... it is beaten for some time or thrown repeatedly, and with force, against the rocks, and at the same time moistened with fresh water.

Travels in Greece and Turkey, 1778

Note: Except for the application of fresh water, the identical method was observed by the compiler on Hydra in November 1980. J.G.

Ogden Nash
1902-71

Tell me, O Octopus, I begs
Is those things arms, or is they legs?
I marvel at thee, Octopus
If I were thou, I'd call me us.

The Octopus

D. H. Lawrence
1885-1930

The fish appeared. And what was it? Fried inkpots. A *calamaio* is an inkpot: also it is a polyp, a little octopus which, alas, frequents the Mediterranean and squirts ink if offended. This polyp with its tentacles is cut up and fried, and reduced to the consistency of boiled celluloid.

Sea and Sardinia

Faith Medlin

More recent reports from Hawaii tell of islanders pounding their octopuses throughout the night in old washing machines kept for that purpose.

A Gourmet's Book of Beasts (1975)

OYSTERS

AU NATUREL

Anonymous

According to experts, the oyster
In its shell (or crustacean cloister)
May at any time be
Either a he or a she
Or both, if it should be its choister.

Cited by Geraldine Pascall, *Weekend Australian* (1982)

Lewis Carroll
1832-98

But four young oysters hurried up,
All eager for the treat
Their coats were brushed, their faces washed,
Their shoes were clean and neat —
And this was very odd, because, you know,
They hadn't any feet.

'The Walrus and the Carpenter', *Through the Looking Glass*

William Vaughan

Oysters must not be eaten in those months which, in pronouncing, want the letter R.

Directions for Health (1600)

John Wilson
1785-1854

A month without an R in it has nae richt being in the year.

Noctes Ambrosianae

William Cowper
1731-1800

Ah, hapless wretch! condemn'd to dwell
For ever in my native shell;
Ordain'd to move when others please,
Not for my own content and ease;
But toss'd and buffeted about,
Now *in* the water and now *out*.
'Twere better to be born a stone,
Of ruder shape, and feeling none,
Than with tenderness like mine,
And sensibilities so fine!

The Poet, the Oyster and the Sensitive Plant

E. G. Boulanger Our native [British] species [of oysters] change sex four times in thirteen months ... [Portuguese and American ones] remain either male or female for the whole of their lives ...

'On Oysters' (c.1927)

AND MANKIND

'Saki'
[H. H. Munro]
1870-1916

I think oysters are more beautiful than any religion ... They not only forgive our unkindness to them; they justify it, they incite us to go on being perfectly horrid to them. Once they arrive at the supper table they seem to enter thoroughly into the spirit of the thing. There's nothing in Christianity or Buddhism that quite matches the unselfishness of the oyster.

The Match-Maker

Ogden Nash
1902-71

Drink deep to Uncle Uglug,
That early heroic human;
The first to eat an oyster,
The first to marry a woman ...
'Had he only eaten the woman,
Had he only married the oyster!'

Stag Night, Palaeolithic

| **Jonathan Swift** 1667-1745 | They say oysters are a cruel meat, because we eat them alive; then they are an uncharitable meat, for we leave nothing for the poor; and they are an ungodly meat, because we never say grace. |

Polite Conversation

| **Robert Browning** 1812-89 | Nor brighter was his eye, nor moister Than a too-long opened oyster. |

The Pied Piper

| **Charles Dickens** 1812-70 | 'It's a werry remarkable circumstance, sir . . . that poverty and oysters always seem to go together'. |

Pickwick Papers

| **W. S. Gilbert** 1836-1911 | He had often eaten oysters, but had never had enough. |

'Etiquette', *Bab Ballads*

| **Anonymous** | Let us roister with the oyster — In the shorter days and moister That are brought by brown September, With its roguish final R; For breakfast or supper, On the under shell or upper, Of dishes he's a daisy, And of shellfish he's the star. |

Costermonger's song (mid-19th century)

| **Rima and Richard Collin** | Oysters Rockefeller . . . was invented at Antoine's [New Orleans] around the turn of the century and named for Rockefeller because it was incredibly rich. |

New Orleans Cookbook (1979)

Note: The oysters for this dish are in the half-shell, set in rock salt, and each topped with a sauce of butter, spinach, watercress, parsley, shallot tops, celery, marjoram, basil, salt, pepper, cayenne, anise seed and Pernod, then baked in an oven at 260°C for 14 to 16 minutes. *J.G.*

LOCALITY

| **F. Marian McNeill** | . . . ample testimony to the quality of 'natives' bred in the once renowned oyster beds of the Firth of Forth . . . (included on the menu of a royal |

banquet at Stirling Castle in 1594 at the baptism of Prince Henry, elder brother of Charles I).

The Scots Kitchen (1929)

Anthony Burgess

Australian seafood is pregnant with wholesome concupiscience: Aphrodite laughs in every oyster.

Press comment (1970)

Malcolm Holland

Tell any Aussie worth his thongs that his beloved Sydney rock oyster is second-rate and you will be told in no uncertain terms to clam up and crawl back into your shell. But Mr Andrew Wong [manager of the Japanese Shin Ju restaurant in Sydney] says, '... Australian oysters just fall apart when you barbecue them ... Japanese oysters retain their flavour and do not dry out when put on the hot plate ...'

'Faced With Competition Our Oysters Fall Apart', *Weekend Australian* (1985)

Anonymous

The Sydney rock oyster has been hailed ... as the most succulent morsel ever to be picked from the sea ... Picky Sydneysiders even insist they be so fresh that they flinch when the lemon juice is applied ... It therefore comes as a great shock to have a Sydney ... owner of a Japanese restaurant declare the local product to be inferior ... This turncoat — who probably barracks for the West Indies cricket team — flies dozen of Japanese oysters ... to Australia each week and serves them to his unsuspecting customers.

Enough! The Japanese already dominate our car market, we take our holiday snaps with Japanese cameras, we watch and listen to cricket on Japanese television sets and radios, we even tell the time with Japanese watches — but Japanese oysters: is nothing sacred?

Boycott the Nipponese mollusc!

Editorial, 'A Slippery Debate', *Weekend Australian* (1985)

Rima and Richard Collin

In Louisiana, salt waters from the Gulf of Mexico ... give our Plaquemines Parish oysters a special taste we call 'salty' ... New Orleans has always had such an abundance of oysters that mid-nineteenth century city directories listed eight or ten restaurants specialising in cooked oyster dishes, and three pages of oyster houses or bars. Oysters Rockefeller . . . grew out of *escargots bourgignons*. Many of us still delight in what might be called an oyster orgy . . . a dozen or two on the half-shell, followed by a plate of fried, then some Rockefellers and some Bienvilles, and perhaps a few *en brochette* for dessert.

The New Orleans Cookbook (1979)

Sallust
186-34 B.C.¿

The poor Britons, there is some good to them after all — they produce an oyster.

In one of his *Histories* (c.50 B.C.)

SHEER GLUTTONY

Geraldine Pascall

The oyster farmers' lunch [in Sydney, Australia] is more a matter of booze, bleating and burlesque. Can familiarity make them exempt?

'Indulgence', *Australian* (1982)

Anonymous

. . . an individual . . . once made a bet that he would eat twelve dozen oysters, washed down by twelve glasses of champagne . . . while the cathedral clock was striking twelve. He won his bet by placing a dozen fresh oysters in twelve wine glasses, and having swallowed the oysters, he washed down each dozen with a glass of Champagne. I should not have mentioned this disgusting feat, but to add that he felt no evil effects . . .

The Oyster (1863)

AND HEALTH

Anonymous

An optimist looks at an oyster and expects a pearl. A pessimist does the same and expects ptomaine poisoning.

Geraldine Pascall, op. cit.

Lt-Col. Newnham-Davis

The great catastrophe of my life . . . was that the first oyster I ate was a bad one.

Gourmets Guide to London (n.d.)

Anonymous

At the period of a lady's married life when nausea is prevalent, a few fresh oysters, taken raw in

their own liquor with no addition but a little pepper, and a fairy slice of French roll or other lighter
bread, stops the feeling of sickness, and keeps up
the stamina unimpaired.

The Oyster (1863)

PARROTS

Anonymous

It is said that the way to cook a galah [pink-
breasted cockatoo] is to put the bird and a rock
into a pot and bring to the boil. Continue cooking.
When the rock is soft enough to eat, throw away
the galah and eat the rock.

Australian bush cooking advice

Mrs L. Rawson

Parrot soup: Pluck and clean 10-12 parrots and just
cover them in a pot with cold water. Simmer 3-4
hours, strain off the liquor, and thicken it with a
little cornflour or arrowroot, and flavour it with
salt, pepper, and spice to taste. The parrots can be
sent to the table as they are, or served with melted
butter.

Mrs Lance Rawson's Cookery Book and Household Hints
(1878)

Note: Personal experience with galahs and other parrots,
sometimes shot after the wheat harvest when they assume pest proportions, was to skin them and then
marinade them in red wine, oil and spices for up to
forty-eight hours in a refrigerator, before casseroling
until tender. *J.G.*

PÂTÉ DE FOIE GRAS

Sydney Smith
1771-1845

His idea of heaven is eating *pâtés de foie gras* to the
sound of trumpets.

Cited by Hesketh Pearson in *The Smith of Smiths*
(1934)

Jean-Paul Aron

[Jean Clause, chef to] Contades, in 1762 [created]
the first *foie gras de Strasbourg*.

The Art of Eating in France (1975)

Andre Launay	Rare, smooth, with a melting quality possessing a strong yet delicate aroma, whose lingering taste is fully savoured by the palate . . . food of the gods, brings that touch of heavenly perfection and that unparalleled enjoyment of a delicacy to the French culinary art, without which it would remain incomplete! . . . An experiment in Ambrosia . . .

Caviare and After (1964) |
| **Carol Willson and John Goode** | In Strasbourg our host not only revelled in the local cuisine, but insisted we sample every facet. Within the carved-timber multi-storey La Maison Kammerzell alongside the cathedral, we were introduced into the natural history of *foie gras* — its production, preparation and consumption. Only there did we learn that it won't travel (because it must be cooked at too low a temperature for health regulations) and to enjoy it fully, you must place a morsel on the tongue and just let it dissolve — a sensation that can be compared only to absorbing ocietrova caviar on the Russian railway restaurant car en route from Helsinki to Leningrad.

'If it's herring, this must be Holland', *Financial Review* (1985) |

PHEASANT

Brillat-Savarin 1755-1826	The pheasant is an enigma whose secret meaning is known only to the initiate . . . when eaten within three days after its death, has nothing distinguishing about it. It is neither as delicate as a pullet, nor as savorous as a quail. At its peak of ripeness . . . its flesh is tender, highly flavoured, and sublime, at once like domestic fowl and wild game. This peak is reached when it begins to decompose . . .

Physiologie du Goût |
| **Ninette Lyon** | Pheasants are best eaten before they are 15 months old. See that . . . the pinions and breastbone [are] supple, and . . . the tail feathers do not pull out to easily. The spurs should be short and rounded (after a year they become pointed, and later hard and ragged). The first wingtip feather, |

which is pointed in the young bird and later rounded, also gives an indication of age. An infallible guide to a yearling pheasant is the upper part of the beak which, in a young bird, is flexible. Hens [are] moister and more delicately flavoured. The feet of a young hen are smooth and slender.

Chicken and Game trans. Peggie Benton (1966)

PIG

Noel Coward
1899-1973

Any part of piggy
Is quite all right with me.
Ham from Wesphalia, ham from Parma,
Ham as lean as the Dalai Lama,
Ham from Virginia, ham from York,
Trotters, sausage, hot roast pork.
Crackling crisp for my teeth to grind on,
Bacon with or without the rind on.
Though humanitarian
I'm not vegetarian.
I'm neither crank nor prude nor prig
And though it may sound infra dig.
Any part of darling pig
Is perfectly fine with me.

Any Part of Piggy

Ogden Nash
1902-71

The pig, if I am not mistaken,
Supplies us sausage, ham, and bacon.
Let others say his heart is big —
I call it stupid of the pig.

The Pig

Jane Grigson

It could be said that European civilisation — and Chinese ... too — has been founded on the pig ... delightful when cooked or cured, from his snout to his tail.

Charcuterie and French Pork Cookery (1967)

PORK

Laurens van der Post

Pork [as cooked in Portuguese Africa] is subjected to some form of marinating. One favourite, used as much in Madeira as it is in Mozambique, consists basically of dry Madeira and wine vinegar combined in equal proportions. Salt, pepper, pounded garlic cloves, sweet red peppers and bay leaf are added, and the pork steaks are cut with a good fringe of lard, and are left to soak in the marinade for eight hours . . . drained and fried . . . [served with] a generous amount of fresh orange juice, laced with dry Madeira . . .

First Catch Your Eland (1977)

William Cowper
1731-1800

Thus says the prophet of the Turk:
Good mussulman, abstain from pork;
There is a part in ev'ry swine
No friend or follower of mine
May taste, what ere his inclination . . .
But for one piece they thought it hard
From the whole hog to be debarr'd . . .
With sophistry their sauce they sweeten,
Till quite from tail to snout 'tis eaten.

Love of the World Reproved

Charles Lamb
1775-1834

There is no flavour comparable, I will contend, to that of the crisp, tawny, well-watched, not over-roasted *crackling*, as it is well called — the very teeth are invited to their share of the pleasure at this banquet in overcoming the coy, brittle resistance . . .

'A Dissertation Upon Roast Pig', *Essays of Elia*

Richard Fields

. . . Lund University [Sweden] passed a thesis proving that if you cook pork chops too long they become tough and unpalatable . . . Ms Stina Fjeeler-Modic . . . devoured 4000 cutlets during a five-year project in which she concluded it was undesirable for a chop to be more than 2cm thick or to stand in the pan more than three minutes after frying . . . taxpayers are not infuriated by this dubious use of money . . . the theses are far more amusing than what frequently passes for enter-tainment in Sweden.

'Doctor of pork chops but no mention of indigestion', *Australian* (1985)

QUAIL

Henry Smith Stuffed, cooked and dressed in aspic, they are much sought after at hunt and country balls. How many present-day debutantes have ever set eyes on one?

The Romans rather feared quails, believing that they caused epileptic fits. Not so the Greeks, who devoured them in large quantities.

The Master Book of Poultry and Game (1960)

Ninette Lyon In spite of, or perhaps because of their fiery spirit and desolate voices, a French doctor in the sixteenth century suggested that husbands and wives who wished to be adored by their spouses should tear the hearts from a pair of quail and lay them on their own — male to female and vice versa. This would ensure a devoted union.

Chicken and Game, trans. Peggie Benton (1966)

RABBIT

Anonymous For rabbits young and rabbits old
For rabbits hot and rabbits cold
For rabbits tender, rabbits tough,
We thank Thee Lord, we've had enough

Country verse, cited by Frank Muir in *The Frank Muir Book* (1976)

Note: Since the advent and introduction of myxomatosis, no Australians have been able to echo this lament. Those available are 'farmed', and exceptionally expensive.

H. D. Williamson Underground mutton [rabbit] to a rabbit-trapper should be as pig-flesh to a Mohammedan.

The Sunlit Plain (1958)

SALMON

Clark Stillman I like lemon on my salmon,
Some like salmon plain.
It's much the same with women,
By and large and in the main . . .

'Women' (n.d.)

| Andre Launay | Because a salmon is smoked it does not mean that it is preserved. A salmon, correctly smoked, with only a minimum of salt added for preservation, will keep its freshness as long as a bottle of milk . . . and put it back in the refrigerator when not immediately required.
Caviare and After (1964) |

SALMON, CANNED

| Jane Grigson | . . . we do not always have to eat it out of tins — which can change its nature completely, from the noble to mere pink protein.
Fish Cookery (1973) |

SAUSAGES

| Apicius | Recipe 60: *Botellum* — little sausage
Botellum is made of hard-boiled yolks of egg, chopped pignoli nuts, onions and leeks, raw ground pine, fine pepper. Stuff in casings and cook in broth and wine.

Possibly the first published sausage recipe
From *Apicius Cookery and Dining in Imperial Rome*, trans. Joseph Dommers Vehling (1936) |

| David Mabey | There isn't any meat in a Glamorgan sausage. It is made from cheese mixed with breadcrumbs, herbs, chopped leek or onion . . . The mixture is bound with the yolk of egg, and formed into sausage shapes, rolled in flour and then dipped in egg white, which forms the 'skin'. Finally they are covered with breadcrumbs, fried and eaten hot with potatoes . . . Tomato sausages . . . sound like a joke . . . I saw them in Carlisle.
In Search of Food (1978) |

| Sir A. P. Herbert | A highbrow is the kind of person who looks at a sausage and thinks of Picasso.
The Highbrow |

| Anonymous | Cambridge [gave the world] science and a sausage. |

Sausages, possibly more than any other item of food, seem to attract nicknames.

Dorris McFerran Townsend

Try that homely but delicious British dish, bangers'n'mash: fluffy mashed potatoes with precooked little fresh pork sausage links buried in them.

The Cook's Companion (1978)

Clifford

'Sausages are snags' (a highly important part of the Australian diet)

Send her down, Hughie (1968)

David Mabey

One small firm which produces sausages in Kent advertises them as 'Kent Korkers' as opposed to 'bangers' . . .

In Search of Food (1978)

SHEEP

Thomas Peacock
1785-1866

The mountain sheep are sweeter,
But the valley sheep are fatter;
We therefore deemed it meeter
To carry off the latter.

The Misfortunes of Elphin (1823)

SNAKE

J. D. Lang

. . . the steam from the roasting snakes was by no means unsavoury and the flesh delicately white . . . it was not unpalatable . . . although rather fibrous and stringy, like lung fish. Mr Wade observed that it reminded him of the taste of eels.

Account of a bush picnic in the 1840s

Faith Medlin

Rattlesnake meat has served as emergency rations for pioneers . . . Any prejudice a novice eater may have . . . is usually overcome when the meat is tasted. Chroniclers over three centuries have compared the flavour to eel, canned tuna, frog, tortoise, chicken ... or rabbit. Rattlesnake meat has appeared on menus as 'prairie eel' ... When properly cooked, the enormous boa and anaconda of tropical America are considered superior to rattlesnake.

Recipes from Africa and India recommend that a python be curried.

'Rattlesnake', *A Gourmet's Book of Beasts* (1975)

TESTICLES

John Goode
We were intrigued to discover the identity of 'ox delicacies' [at the Szechuan Restaurant in the Ambassador Hotel, Taipei] used both in soup and fried. Our initial inquiries seemed beyond the staff's knowledge of English. However, next morning, there was a discretely folded illustration of an ox in our pigeonhole. It listed the various cuts. On it, in ink, was a circled area behind the skirt with the words 'Right here!' All was revealed. The French know them as *animelles*, the Americans as 'fry'. To an Australian butcher, they are testicles. Unfortunately time prevented us from trying them ...

Twenty Great Dishes from Taiwan (1983)

William Verral
Lambs-stones marinaded and fry'd with parsley ... the French are more modest, and give it a prettier name — *Des alumelles d'agneaux.*

The Complete System of Cookery (1759)

TURBOT

Martial
43-104
However wide the dish that bears the turbot, yet the turbot is wider than the dish.

Epigrams

T. E. Welby
'Turbot, Sir,' said the waiter, placing before me two fishbones, two eyeballs, and a bit of black mackintosh.

'The Dinner Knell' (n.d.)

Brillat-Savarin
1755-1826

... the largest and, if not the most delicate, at least the most flavourful of our domestic birds ... A truffled turkey! ... its restorative juices have more than once lighted up a face until then pre-eminently and discreetly diplomatic ... While I was in Hartford, in Connecticut, I had the good luck to kill a wild turkey ... Only a hunter will understand the bliss such a lucky shot gave me. I picked up the superb winged creature and stood admiring him ... for a good quarter of an hour.

Physiologie du Goût

'Cassandra'
[William
Connor]

What a shocking fraud the turkey is. In life preposterous, insulting — that foolish noise they make ... In death — unpalatable ... practically no taste except a dry fibrous flavour reminiscent of a mixture of warmed up plaster-of-paris and horsehair. The texture is like wet sawdust and the whole vast feathered swindle has the piquancy of a boiled mattress.

'Talking Turkey', *Daily Mirror* (1953)

Turbot ... two eyeballs and a bit of black mackintosh.

TURTLE

Thomas Hood
1799-1845

'Of all the things I ever swallow —
Good well-dressed turtle beats them hollow —
It almost makes me wish, I vow,
To have *two* stomachs, like a cow!'
And lo! as with the cud, an inward thrill
Upheaved his waistcoat and disturb'd his frill,
His mouth was oozing, and he work'd his jaw —
'I almost think I could eat one raw'.

The Turtle

Andre Launay

... getting the meat from a turtle is similar to
decarbonising an engine.

Caviare and After (1964)

Robert Browning
1812-89

Save when at noon, his paunch grew mutinous,
For a plate of turtle green and glutinous.

The Pied Piper of Hamelin

VEAL

Alexander Pope
1688-1744

Take a knuckle of veal,
You may buy it, or steal,
In a few pieces cut it,
In a stewing pan put it,
Salt pepper and mace
Must season this knuckle . . .
In a boiling hot kettle,
And there let it be,
(Mark this doctrine I teach)
About — let me see —
Thrice as long as you preach . . .*

'Receipt for Stewing Veal' (attrib.)
*Estimated at four hours

VENISON

Peter Pindar
1738-1819

One cut from ven'son to the heart can speak
Stronger than ten quotations from the Greek.

Bozzy and Piozzi

WHITEBAIT

John Lawson-Ward

At Fort Lamy, in the Lake Chad territories ... whitebait were served *a l'anglaise*, with slice of bread and butter ... some ... preferred them with a thin vinegar sauce, rather like Worcester, but mixed with oil and with a suggestion of garlic. I was surprised to see whitebait, and was told that they flourish in the salt waters of Lake Chad; they were somewhat bigger and less tasteful than our home [English] variety.

'Fort Lamy Menu' (1943)

Carol Willson and John Goode

For reasons best known to themselves the bulk of New Zealand restaurants apparently sell whitebait only in fritters. So far as we are concerned, whitebait have far too delicate a flavour to be swamped by any batter.

The Original Australia and New Zealand Fish Cookbook (1979)

WOODCOCK

[¿] Fonssagrives

I consider that woodcock is difficult to digest, indeed, harmful to health especially when it is prepared as a *salmis*.

Cited by Prosper Montagné in *Larousse Gastronomique*

Henry Smith

Woodcock has been described as the queen of the game birds, and has excited the pens of French gourmets to the highest raptures ... treasured for its unusual flavour.

The Master Book of Poultry and Game, n.d. (c.1960)

Godard d'Aucour

When a woodcock is reduced to a purée
Prepared by a skilful art,
This dish, so rare, and not less precious,
Should only be served at the banquets of gods.

Cited by Montagné, Op. cit.

WOOD-PIGEONS

Martial
43-104

Wood-pigeons check and blunt the manly powers: let him not eat this bird who wishes to be amorous.

Epigrams

Lilli Gore

In England, the abundance and greed of the wood pigeon has exposed him to death all the year round ... they consume brussels sprouts as well as corn, beech nuts and acorns — and ... make plump gamey birds. In France they are bred ... for the table and often eaten at four weeks of age, when they are known as pigeonneaux — squabs ...

Game Cooking (1974)

YABBIES

Edward E. Morris

YABBY, *n.* properly *Yappée*, aboriginal name for a small crayfish found in water-holes in many parts of Australia.

Austral English (1898)

L. H. Dalziel

A swaggy from Toon-bloody-gabby
Was savaged to death by a yabby.
So unique was his fate
That his sorrowing mate
Had him buried in Westminster Abbey.

Australasian Post (1979)

Peter Olszewski

'I heard the French reckon the yabby is a gourmet food' ... 'Not only the French. The Swedes, most Europeans and some Americans ... It's being farmed now, and most of the big names in the cookery business have recognised the yabby's gourmet quality'.

Salute to the Humble Yabby (1980)

FLAVOURS AND SEASONINGS

ANISETTE LIQUEUR

Elizabeth David

... anisette is, improbably but incontrovertibly, a quite magical ingredient in fish dishes and sauces. You rarely need more than a teaspoonful, you add it at the absolute final moment of cooking, you do not blaze it (at least I do not), you treat it simply as a seasoning ... its concentrated, pungent-sweet and aromatic qualities give a lift such as could hardly be achieved with a mountain of fennel stalks or seeds used in the preparation of the initial stock ...

'Whisky in the Kitchen', in *The Compleat Imbiber* (1963)

CHILLIES

[¢] Ward

The quantity of chile disposed of was really prodigious; wagons laden with it, drawn each by six oxen, were arriving hourly [at the market in Zacatecas] ... piles of capsicum, sufficient to excoriate the palates of half London, vanishing in the course of a few minutes.

Ward's Mexico

Diana Kennedy

Chillies are indigenous to Mexico and played an important part in the cuisine long before the Spaniards arrived ... there are roughly two hundred different types ... over a hundred of which are to be found in Mexico ... Each chilli has its own character as well, a definite flavour and a degree of piquancy — from the large, mild green chilli from Magdalena in Sonora to the most fiery of all, the *chille habanero* of Yucatan. And chillies on the same plant can vary from mild to hot. Many . . . can be used fresh or dried . . .

The Cuisines of Mexico (1972)

Clement Freud I first came across [chilli con carne] in Mexico City, where I ordered it because of some dimly remembered Hemingway reference. I took a forkful of the stuff and then ordered six bottles of cold beer in quick succession . . . I mentioned to the proprietor that it might be advisable to warn strangers about his speciality . . . the ratio . . . turned out to be a pound of meat to a pound of chilli peppers. Had I wanted *carne* with a little chilli, he said, there was an American place just down the road.

Freud on Food (1978)

COMFREY

Stephen Osborne (Coroner in Auckland, NZ) Paul Edward Neutze, 23, of Wellington [New Zealand] died on 31 October 1985 from liver failure caused by eating a medicinal herb . . . a large dietary intake of comfrey . . . This young man had obviously not learnt the virtue of moderation in all things. Comfrey might be innocuous, even beneficial in moderation, but lethal otherwise.

'Stay in Touch', *Sydney Morning Herald* (1986)

CHUTNEY

John F. Mackay All Things chickeny and mutt'ny
Taste better far when served with chutney.
This is the mystery eternal:
Why didn't Major Grey make Colonel?

Cited in *New York Times* (1984)

Dharamjit Singh There is *chatni*, or chutney, made with vinegar, sugar and spices; there are fresh chutneys which will keep several days in a cool place; and there are *achars*, pickled fruits, vegetables, meat, game or fish given a long marination in oil. Only the chutneys are known outside India.

Indian Cookery (1970)

GARLIC

G. S. Whittet

Breakfast, dinner, supper, tea —
When e'er Maria eats it;
In everything she says to me
She — so to speak — repeats it.
  Garlic

Alexis Soyer

Garlic . . . was a God of Egypt. The Greeks held it
in horror. It was part of their military food —
hence came the proverb 'Eat neither garlic nor
beans' [abstain from war and law] . . . It was a
prevailing opinion that the effects of foul air were
neutralised by garlic . . . no doubt, this idea . . .
made reapers and peasants use it so lavishly.
  Pantropheon (1977)

**Alun Gwyne
Jones**

Consider for a moment the French —
I mean, of course, the people themselves, not the
    stench
Of garlic in their underground trains . . .
  Double Entente Cordiale

P. B. Shelley
1792-1822

There are two Italies — the one is the most sublime and lovely contemplation that can be conceived by the imagination of man; the other is the most degraded, disgusting and odious. What do you think? Young women of rank actually eat — you will never guess what — garlick!

Letter

GARUM

Alexis Soyer

The Greeks called the shrimp *garos*, the Romans *garus*: it may be hence supposed that garum had originally for basis the flesh of shrimps . . . It was afterwards composed of other fish . . . they macerated the intestines of fish in water, saturated with salt, until putrefaction began . . . then added parsley and vinegar. The expensive garum was especially esteemed when it came from Spain . . . This brine became exquisite, and obtained an exorbitant price when made from the liver of anchovies macerated in vinegar, pepper, salt, parsley, garlic, white wine and sweet herbs.

The Pantropheon (1853)

HERBS

Rudyard Kipling
1865-1936

Excellent herbs had our fathers of old,
Excellent herbs to ease their pain;
Alexander and marigold,
Eyebright, orris and elecampane,
Basil, rocket, valerian, rue,
(Almost singing themselves they run,)
Vervain, dittany, call-me-to-you,
Cowslip, melilot, rose of the sun,
Anything green that grew out of the mould
Was an excellent herb to our fathers of old.

Cited by Leyel and Hartley, *The Gentle Art of Cookery*

Andre Launay

In the early fifteenth century . . . the German Emperor insisted on having his girls rubbed with spices so that he could choose the one whose breath smelt most of Tarragon, or Coriander, depending on the time of day . . . At Versailles,

under Louis XIV, they went quite mad . . . by per-
fuming all their food. Orris root and rosewater
was freely sprinkled on meats, pastries and pies,
walnuts were flavoured with musk, cream
whipped up with ambergris and eggs bathed in
scents.

Note: Musk and ambergris were considered to be
aphrodisiacs. *J. G.*

    Caviare and After (1964)

HORSERADISH

Yann Lovelock

[Horseradish] is most popular in northern countries . . . Britain, Germany and Alsace — where it
was once so popular that there were very few
meals where it was not present, either raw as an
appetiser, or cooked like a vegetable . . . *Eutrema
wasabi* is a Japanese relation cultivated for the sake
of its roots, which are used as a condiment.

    The Vegetable Book (1972)

Note: It is also used extensively in a cream sauce in
Scandinavian countries. *J. G.*

**Alexandre
Dumas**
1802-70

Horseradish has the same disadvantage as the
French turnip. It is equally apt to bring on
flatulence, causes a heaving of the stomach and
even provokes headaches, when too much of it is
eaten.

    Dumas on Food, translated by Alan and Jane Davidson
    (1979)

MACE

Sir Harry Luke

. . . mace — that aesthetically beautiful by-
product of the nutmeg tree, a network husk of
deep and brilliant lacquer-red while it is still fresh
on the nut — enriches thick soups, and the stock-
pot generally, with its singularly piquant aroma.

    The Tenth Muse (1954)

MINT

X. M. Boulestin . . . mint is not cultivated in French gardens. I did not know then that there are many kinds of mints, and that the one which is used for the sauce does not grow wild.

Myself, My Two Countries (1920s)

Tom Stobart . . . mints with the finest flavour are not the commonly-grown spearmints, but the large, woolly-leaved apple mints . . . The woolly texture disappears on chopping . . . Both spearmint and mint sauce were introduced to Britain by the Romans . . . in India, mint is ground with coconut, and forms the basis of chutneys which will also contain onion, green chilli, green mango and other substances.

Herbs, Spices and Flavourings (1977)

MUSTARD

Anonymous I make my profit not by the mustard people use, but from what they leave on their plates.

Attributed to George Colman, founder of Colman's Mustard

YES SIR, MR COLMAN WILL BE PLEASED.!

Madhur Jaffrey Mustard seeds are the Jekyll and Hyde of the spice world. If allowed to pop quickly in hot oil, they remain innocently mild and nutty. But just grind them up for Bengali-style prawns and they go tingling up the nose like champagne bubbles.

'Making Magic with Spices', *The Times* (1982)

Tom Stobart Mixing [mustard powder] with boiling water . . . kills the enzymes and produces a milder but bitter mustard . . . To preserve mustard's pungency in cooked dishes, add late and cook gently.

Herbs, Spices and Flavourings (1977)

NUTMEG

Aaron Hill But be rough as nutmeg-graters,
1685-1750 And the rogues will obey you well.

Verses Written on a Window in Scotland

Pamela Westland In the twelfth century, the streets of Rome were fumigated with nutmeg before the coronation procession of Emperor Henry VI passed by.

The Encyclopedia of Spices (1979).

Joseph Addison The present Emperor of Persia denominates him-
1672-1719 self 'the sun of glory and the nutmeg of delight'.

Spectator (1711)

PAPRIKA

George Lang Hungary was unquestionably the first to use pow-dered paprika in pure form . . . In Turkey, Central and South America it was only used whole, added to other foods. The Spaniards mixed it with other spices, kneading it into a flat pancake, which they dried . . . and then ground . . . the Hungarians hit on the holy trinity of lard, onion and pure ground paprika . . . the base of virtually unlimited taste combinations.

The Cuisine of Hungary (1971)

PARSLEY

Ogden Nash
1902-71

Parsley is gharsley.
  'Further Reflections on Parsley'

Yann Lovelock

Parsley wound around a carrot means fecundity. I imagine that the symbology has Freudian implications especially as parsley seems to have some connection with lust and lovemaking.
  The Vegetable Book (1972)

PEPPER

**Pamela
Westland**

... the black pepper indigenous to India features in early Brahmanic texts, where it is mentioned in the treatment of [many] complaints ... always the world's most sought-after spice.
  The Encyclopedia of Spices (1979)

POPPY SEEDS

Tom Stobart

In Europe and the Middle East, the main use of poppy seed is in confectionery. The flavour, when baked, is pleasantly nutty ... Poppy seed is used in curries, where its function is partly for flavouring and partly to improve the texture and thicken the gravy ... [it] is also an important source of oil ... known in France as *olivette*.
  Herbs, Spices and Flavourings (1977)

Walter James

Galen described both the seed and the poppies from which it was gathered; Gerrard, in his Elizabethan English herbal, tells us ... it was 'often used in comfits, served at table with other junketing dishes'.
  Antipasto (1957)

ROSEMARY

Elizabeth David

Many Italians stuff joints of lamb and pork with rosemary ... The meat is drowned in the acrid

taste . . . and the spiky little leaves get stuck in
your teeth. Once, in an out-of-doors Capri café, I
saw an old woman basting her fish . . . with a
branch of rosemary dipped in olive oil. That's
about as much rosemary as, personally, I want.

Spices, Salt and Aromatics in the English Kitchen (1971)

William
Shakespeare
1564-1616

There's rosemary, that's for remembrance.
Hamlet

SAGE

Thomas Cogan

Of all the garden herbs, none is of greater virtue
than sage.
The Haven of Health (1596)

Rita Erlich &
Dennis Proctor

For life everlasting remember
Eat plenty of sage in November
Two in the Kitchen (1981)

SALT

John Florio
c.1553-1625

Salt seasons all things.
Second Frutes

Elizabeth de
Grey

Forget not the salt.
A True Gentlewoman's Delight (1653)

Cassiodorus
468-568

In the famous Venetia, fish alone is abundant; rich
and poor live there on equal terms . . . All your
rivalry is expended in your salt works; in place of
ploughs and sickles you turn your drying pans,
and hence comes all your gain . . . It may well be
that there are some men who seek gold, but there
lives no man who does not need salt, which
seasons our food.
Letter to the Maritime Tribunes of Venice, A.D. 500

SPICES

Sir Harry Luke And what a rich, evocative aroma they have, those ancient vaulted bazaars of Aleppo and Damascus and the Old City of Jerusalem, of Qazvin and Meshed and Isfahan, as you approach the streets of the vendors of spices. Here you inhale an amalgam of all the aboriginal savours and smells of the Orient . . .

The Tenth Muse (1954)

Note: A similar sensation could be experienced late in 1982 in the Indian quarter around Leboh Ampang in Kuala Lumpur. *J.G.*

John Goode There's a lot more to spices than food flavourings . . . they've been used as medicines and money, love potions and deodorants. The Romans prescribed cinnamon for head colds and cardamom to treat piles. In the Middle Ages, the spice trade amassed fortunes, spurred explorations and even caused wars.

'The World for a Pinch of Spice' *Vogue Living* (1982)

TARRAGON

Brian Hill Catherine of Aragon
Stole a quart jar of Tarragon.
'It's the last in the bin,'
She informed Anne Boleyn.
'It's lovely, give me more!'
Entreated Jane Seymour,
Which made Anne of Cleves
Spill a lot down her sleeves.
'Not for me, I'm a coward!'
Said Catherine Howard.
But Catherine Parr
Drank the rest of the jar.

'Undiscovered History' (n.d.)

TOMATO SAUCE

David Dale   If you're the sort of person who buys a bottle of
tomato sauce every fortnight, your life's an open
book ... you do like your brand of sauce.
Wouldn't change, unless the price of one of the
other brands dropped dramatically ... You put
sauce on your steak, your chops, your sausages,
your eggs, your chips, your fish fingers and, of
course, your pies. Your kids take tomato sauce
sandwiches to school, and have been known to
put it on their ice cream.

Sun-Herald (1974)

WORCESTERSHIRE SAUCE

David Mabey   In 1823, Mr William Perrins, a chemist from Eve-
sham, formed a partnership with Mr John
Wheeley Lea ... in Worcester. In 1835 Lord
Sandys, returning ... from India, walked into Lea
and Perrins shop with a recipe ... acquired ... in
the East. In 1838 they started to manufacture it on
a commercial scale, but were very careful to keep
the essential details of the process [quantities of
ingredients and maturation period] ... a secret for
150 years.

In Search of Food (1978)

'Wyvern'   I denounce 'Worcester Sauce' and 'Tapp's Sauce'
[Col. Kenney-   as agents too powerful to be trusted to the hands
Herbert]   of the native cook.

Culinary Jottings for Madras (1885)

PRODUCTS OF THE VINE

BRANDY AND COGNAC

Rudyard Kipling
1865-1936

Brandy for the parson,
'Baccy for the clerk;
Laces for a lady, letters for a spy,
Watch the wall, my darling, while the gentlemen
go by!
'A Smugglers' Song'

**Horace
Annesley A.
Vachell**

There is enough Napoleon brandy in novels to
float a battleship.
Cited in 'Some Novelists and Wine' (c.1943)

O. W. Holmes
1809-94

If wine tells truth — and so have said the wise —
It makes me laugh to think how brandy lies!
'The Banker's Secret'

Mike Lawrence

Cognac may be brandy, but all brandy isn't cognac! ... Some [brandies] are drinkable, mostly as
a mixer, others are best used for removing tar
stains from Volkswagens or stripping paint from
old wooden dressers ... Cognac, however, is that
special smooth, fragrant brandy produced in
south-western France in an area defined by law in
1909.
'Very Superior Old Present', *Epicurean* (1981)

Cyril Ray

Cognac, ousted from its role as a mixer, in 'B & S',
made a magnificent come-back as the lordliest of
after-dinner drinks, in Britain actually challenging
vintage port ... as whisky had so successfully
challenged brandy for preprandial honours.
Spirits and Liqueurs (1977)

CHAMPAGNE

OPINIONS

Raymond Postgate

... the king of wines — champagne. There are other sparkling wines, but there is nothing much to say about them except that they are very good for parties, taste very much alike (except the nasty ones . . .) and are cheaper.

'A Short Account of Wines', *Lilliput* (1954)

Frank Margan

I have heard it described as 'the rich man's Enos'.

The Grape and I (1969)

G. Bernard Shaw
1856-1950

I'm only a beer teetotaller, not a champagne teetotaller.

Candida

HEART OF THE MATTER

Edward Hyams

Don Perignon (1638-1715), a monk at the Benedictine Abbey of Hautvilliers, made champagne a manageable wine for commerce.

Dionysus (1965)

Cyril Ray

... the most famous, certainly the most festive, wine in the world comes from some 40,000 acres [16,200 ha] . . . in the department of Marne . . .

The Wines of France (1976)

André Simon

Champagne made from a blend of Black Pinot [and Chardonnay] — some from the Montage de Rheims vineyards, some from the Valley of the Marne and some from the Côtes des Blancs — is a much better wine, more balanced, more complete, more lasting . . . gaining power as well as charm with age.

The History of Champagne (1962)

Cyril Ray

Madame Bollinger and her colleagues . . . treat their equally well-bred wine with a less ostentatious — with a graver — dignity. It is their custom . . . to serve their wine in tall glasses, tulip-shaped ... the *coupé* or *tazza* ... even if it were true that its origin is a set of Sèvres porcelain *tazza* modelled from the breasts of Marie Antoinette, André Simon ... has shown that the *coupé* was designed and first made in England, specifically for champagne, in or about 1663, over a hundred years before Marie Antoinette had any breasts to speak of.

Bollinger (1971)

Eric Quayle

Dressed Salmon in Champaign Wine (as published by Patrick Lambe in *Royal Cookery*, 1710) is one of the earliest recipes we know that makes use of the newly invented champagne ... [it] already bore some resemblance to the sparkling wine we know by that name today. Although historians of the social scene have pronounced that it was probably 'as red as burgundy and as flat as port', in fact, champagne had already paled to 'the colour of a partridge's eye' by the time Lambe's book appeared.

Old Cook Books (1978)

Anton Chekhov
1860-1904

... we prepared ourselves to mark the coming of the New Year with unaccustomed solemnity ... The reason was that we had set by two bottles of Champagne, the real thing, labelled Veuve Clicquot ...

Le Recut d'un Chemineau (1890)

Holly Kerr

Champagne is the wine *par excellence* for celebrations; we need it in defeat and deserve it in victory. None other, it seems, is suitable equally both for an intimate supper and for launching battleships; it can be drunk with cornflakes or with Beef Wellington.

Representing the CIVC in Australia; speech to the French Association of Specialists c.1984.

DISPENSATION AND RESPONSE

Douglas Lamb

It has been said that the final sound from the uncorking of a bottle of Champagne is like the sigh of a contented woman.

Select Wine Club brochure, Sydney, 1981

Frank Harris
1855-1931

... champagne is the most exhilarating change from Bordeaux; it is like the woman of the streets: everybody that can afford it tries it sooner or later, but it has no real attraction. It must be taken in moderation: too much of it is apt to give a bad headache, or worse. Like the woman of the streets, it is always within reach and its price is out of all proportion to its worth.

My Life and Loves

Patrick Forbes

The first morning glass is the best of the whole day.

Champagne (1967)

Horatio Smith
1779-1849

Champagne doth not a Luncheon make
Nor caviare a meal ...

At the Cock Tavern

Laurens van der Post

... a banquet at the Imperial Palace [Addis Abbaba] ... with the best of dry Champagne served last of all and not spoilt, as it is invariably in the English-speaking world, by appearing at the beginning.

First Catch Your Eland (1977)

Allan Sichel

Of all natural wine aperitifs, Champagne is the champion. Not only does it leave the palate clean, but it revives tired guests or hostesses as quickly as any spirit, and by means of a far more gentle application of alcohol to the system ... indispensible to the success of a dinner party ... In France there are many who like to end a meal with medium-dry Champagne. Personally I can do without the rather high acidity ...

Penguin Book of Wines (1971)

Francis Bacon
1909-

Champagne is for real friends, real pain for sham friends.

Cited by Judy Brittain in 'On Air, The Houses of Champagne', British *Vogue* (1978)

R. S. Surtees
1803-64

Champagne certainly gives one werry gentleman-ly ideas, but for a continuance, I don't know but I should prefer mild *hale*.

Jorrock's Jaunts and Jollities

. . . AND MIXES

Cyril Ray   Buck's Fizz . . . consists of two parts of champagne to one of fresh orange juice, served very
cold in a tall, tulip-shaped glass (at Buck's Club in
London).
Op. cit.

JOIE DE VIVRE and OTHER OBSERVATIONS

Cyril Ray   William Younger (*Gods, Men and Wine*, 1966)
found what might well be the first recorded in-
stance of [champagne] being drunk out of a lady's
slipper — in *The Connoisseur* of 6 June 1754. The
lady was no better than she should be: I hope the
wine was.
Bollinger (1971)

Madame de   Champagne is the only wine to leave a woman
Pompadour   beautiful after drinking.
1721-64   Attrib.

Walter James   A well bred old champagne has points in common with a well-bred old man. Youth's ebullient,
slightly vulgar froth and turbulence have gone,
leaving a little spring of subdued bubbles rising
slowly through an old-gold liquor in the manner
of a dry but gentle wit that sometimes sparkles in
mature minds.
Antipasto (1957)

Dorothy Parker   Three be the things I shall ne'er attain:
1893-1967   Envy, content, and sufficient champagne.
'Inventory', *Portable Dorothy Parker* (1944)

CLARET

John Keats   My friends should drink a dozen of Claret on my
1795-1821   Tomb.
To Benjamin Bailey

HIPPOCRAS

Ruth Martin   *Hippocras:* mediaeval wine drink, sweetened with honey, and flavoured with herbs and spices.
International Dictionary of Food and Cooking (1973)

Goodman of Paris   Take a quarter of very fine cinnamon . . . half a quarter of fine flour of cinnamon, an ounce of selected string ginger . . . and an ounce of grain [cardamom], a sixth of nutmegs and galingale . . . pound them all together . . . take a good two ounces of this powder and two quarts of sugar and mix them with a quart of wine . . .
Cited by Tannahill, *Fine Art of Food* (1968)

Reay Tannahill   The name 'hippocras' was derived from the type of strainer used, which was known as Hippocrates' Sleeve.
Op. cit.

MADEIRA

Laurens van der Post   . . . the greatest cooking wine of the world and, were it not so expensive, it would be used very widely.
First Catch Your Eland (1977)

Anonymous   When asked for his opinion of Madeira presented by an East India Company officer, an Asian chief said that he 'thought it a juice extracted from women's tongues and lions' hearts; for, after he drank a sufficient quantity of it, he could talk for ever, and also fight like the devil'.
Tavern Anecdotes (1825)

MALMSEY

Ruth Martin   Sweet dessert wine imported to Britain from Sardinia, Sicily, Madeira and the Canary Islands, and drunk as an *aperitif*; it also replaces Madeira, etc. to flavour sauces, etc.
International Dictionary of Food and Cooking (1973)

William Shakespeare
1564-1616

2nd Murderer: Look behind you, my lord.
1st Murderer: Take that *[Stabs the Duke of Clarence]*, and that:
If all this will not do,
I'll drown you in the malmsey-butt within.

Richard III

MULLED WINES

Jonathan Swift
1667-1745

. . . fine oranges
Well roasted with sugar and wine in a cup
They'll make sweet Bishop* when gentlefolks sup.

Cited in Pamela Westland's *The Encyclopedia of Spices* (1979)
*The Bishop — a famous hot punch based on non-vintage port

John Goode

Although 'to mull' meant to heat and add spice to wine, Shakespeare used the verb to mean 'to stupefy'. And if you happen to have mulled over the foregoing (in America, to mull means to cogitate or ponder), take care that when you put any of the above formulae into practice, you don't end up in a Shakespearean condition.

'Hot Helpers', *Vogue Living* (1981)

OPENING A WINE BOTTLE

Charpentier

[About 1920] I plunged into my cellar, and with the careful, hurried pace of one carrying nitroglycerine out of a burning building, returned with a bottle of Pommard, 1888 . . . I drew that cork so carefully it did not squeak in grief as it was parted from its bottle.

Those Rich and Great Ones (1935)

PORT WINE

Thomas Hood
1799-1845

The Gentleman did take a drop too much . . .
And took more Port than was exactly portable.
The Green Man

George Meredith
1828-1909

An aged Burgundy runs with a beardless Port. I cherish the fancy that Port speaks sentences of wisdom, Burgundy sings the inspired ode.

The Egoist

Walter James

Port joins sweet sherry and muscat to form the terrible trinity of the Australian wine trade, and reflects everything that is bad about it ... because the enormous demand of undiscriminating saloon drinkers, whose simple urge is for something sweet and strong, has given rise to a yearly saccharine deluge pressed out of grapes of the first variety that comes to hand, and bottled and put on the market as soon as the last fermentation bubble has risen.

Wine in Australia (1952)

Charles H. Baker Jr

Port Wine ... Needed in enough unusual cocktails to make it necessary on any fairly well-stocked shelf. Also an essential after coffee in any civilized community

The Gentleman's Companion (1946)

Frank Harris
1855-1931

Port is the woman of forty: stronger, richer, sweeter even than Burgundy; much more body in it but less bouquet; it keeps excellently and ripens with age and can only be drunk freely by youth; in maturity, more than a sip of it is apt to be heavy, and if taken every day it is almost certain to give gout. But if you are vigorous and don't fear the consequences, the best wine in the world is crusted Port, half a century old; it is strong, with divine fragrance — heady, intoxicating — but constant use of it is not to be recommended; it affects the health of even its strongest and most passionate admirers and brings them to premature death.

My Life and Loves

SACK

Alexis Lichine

Canary Sack and Palma Sack (the later from Las Palmas, port of Gran Canaria) made the Spanish islands of Africa famous in the Elizabethan Age

. . . Early name for Sherry . . . afterwards attached to other, comparable, wines . . .

Encyclopedia of Wines and Spirits (1974)

Note: In Henry IV Parts I and 2 Shakespeare, through Falstaff, makes mention of sack and that was obviously sweetened, mixed with eggs and other ingredients to make a punch (q.v.).

**William
Shakespeare
1605-35**

If I had a thousand sons, the first human principle I would teach them should be to forswear thin potations and to addict themselves to sack.
If sack and sugar be a fault, God help the wicked!

Henry IV, Part II

SHERRY

Henry McNulty

Send a Fino to San Lucar de la Barrameda and it will eventually become a Manzanilla ... send a Manzanilla to Jerez and it will become a Fino: such are the mysteries of making wine . . .

'Sherry for a Dry Summer', *Vogue* (1978-79)

Walter James

The citizens of Bristol [England] call sherry 'Bristol milk', through the happy custom of moistening the lips of their newborn babies with the sweet, rich, olorosos which older babes may still purchase under the name Bristol Milk. Oh, to be born in Bristol!

Antipasto (1957)

Stephen Potter

For Home Winemanship, remember that your mainstay is hypnotic suggestion. Suggest some rubbishy sherry, nine bob, is your special pride, and has a tremendously individual taste. Insist on getting it yourself 'from the cellar'. Take about four minutes uncorking it. Say, 'I think decanting destroys it', if you have forgotten or are too bored to decant it.

One-Upmanship (1952)

SPANISH WINES

Quentin Crewe   Spain is a grand country for drinking . . . because
the Spaniards do not approach the matter too rev-
erentially . . . you would never catch the French
calling one of their finest clarets 'Uncle Bill',
which is, after all, the rough equivalent of *Tio
Pepe*.

Quentin Crewe's International Pocket Food Book (1980)

TOKAY

Carol Willson   In one square [of Colmar in Alsace] is a statue of
and John Goode   Baron Schwendi. He was a 16th century general
who brought Tokay vines from Hungary. Today,
Tokay grapes from Alsace are used to make the
only dry Tokay — the ideal complement when
eating *foie gras*.

'Alsace has the best of two worlds', Sun-Herald

George Lang   Perhaps Hungary has the only national anthem
that contains a stanza thanking God for the country's wine. The 1823 poem by Ferenc Kolcsey . . .
contains the lines:

On the grapevines of Tokaj
Thou dripped nectar . . .

. . . the whole history of Hungary is interwoven
with its complex culture of wines, nowhere more
evident than around the hills of Tokaj in the
northeast . . .

The Cuisine of Hungary (1971)

Voltaire   And the yellowish liqueur of Tokay,
1694-1778   While caressing the fibres of the brain,
Carries a fire that generates witticism
As dazzling as the liqueur is light . . .

Cited by Lang, Op. cit

WINE

ITS EFFECT

Pliny the Elder
fl. A.D. 60

In vino veritas (In wine there is truth).
   Natural History

John Pomfret
1667-1702

Wine whets the wit, improves its native force,
And gives pleasant flavour to discourse.
   The Choice

Thomas Bacon

For when the wine is in the wit is out.
   Catechism (n.d.)

Robert Herrick
1591-1674

Brisk methinks I am, and fine,
When I drink my capering wine;
Then to love do I incline,
When I do drink my wanton wine;
And I wish all maidens mine,
When I drink my sprightly wine;
Well I sup, and well I dine,
When I drink my frolic wine;
But I languish, lower, and pine,
When I want my fragrant wine.

   Anacreontic Verse

**Edward
FitzGerald**
1809-83

And much as wine has play'd the Infidel,
And robbed me of my Robe of honour — Well,
I wonder often what the vintners buy
One half so precious as the stuff they sell.
   Rubai'yat of Omar Khayyam

VARIETIES AND PREFERENCE

John Masefield
1878-1967

Oh some are fond of Spanish wine
and some are fond of French.
   Captain Stratton's Fancy

**Raymond
Postgate**

. . . claret has been for little over eight hundred
years the most appreciated wine in England.
   'A Short Account of Wines', *Lilliput* (1954)

Stephen Potter	Winemanship. . . is 'How to talk about wine without knowing a Hock from a Horse's Neck'.
	One Upmanship (1952)
Andre Launay	As far as I am concerned there are only two types of wine, those I like and those I don't like, and it is simply a matter of trial and error to find out which wines you prefer.
	Caviare and After (1964)
Frank Harris 1885-1931	Red Bordeaux . . . is like the lawful wife: an excellent beverage that goes with every dish and enables one to enjoy one's food, and helps one live . . . Moselle is the girl of fourteen to eighteen: light, quick on the tongue with an exquisite evanescent perfume, but little body; it may be used constantly and in quantities, but must be taken young.
	If you prefer real fragrance or bouquet, you must go to a wine with more body in it, such as Burgundy, Chambertin or Musigny. Burgundy I always think of as the woman of thirty: it has more body than claret, is richer, more generous, with a finer perfume; but it is very intoxicating and should be used with self restraint. . .
	My Life and Loves
D. H. Lawrence 1885-1930	The Spanish Wine, my God, it is foul, catpiss is champagne compared, this is the sulphurous urination of some aged horse.
	Letter to Rhys Davis, *The Letters of D. H. Lawrence*
Marcus Clarke 1846-81	No man has the right to inflict bad wine upon his fellow creatures.
	The Peripatetic Philosopher (1869)

PUTTING DOWN

R. H. Barham 1788-1845	I question if keeping does it much good After ten years in the bottle, and three in the wood.
	'The Wedding Day', *Ingoldsby Legends*
J. T. Trowbridge 1827-1916	With years a richer life begins, The spirit mellows:

Ripe age gives tone to violins,
Wine, and good fellows
  Three Worlds

... AND WOMEN

**W. M.
Thackeray
1811-63**

Then sing, as Martin Luther sang,
As Doctor Martin Luther sang:
'Who loves not wine, woman, and song,
He is a fool his whole life long!'
  A Credo

**Lord Byron
1788-1824**

Let us have wine and women, mirth and laughter,
Sermons and soda-water the day after.
  Don Juan

**Edward
FitzGerald
1809-83**

Here with a loaf of bread beneath the bough,
A Flask of Wine, a Book of Verse, and Thou
Beside me singing in the Wilderness —
And Wilderness is Paradise enow.
  Rubai'yat of Omar Khayyam

**John Ray
1628-1705**

Wine and wenches empty men's purses.
  English Proverbs

**Robert Burton
1577-1640**

I may not here omit those two main plagues and
common dotages of human kind, wine and
women, which have infatuated and besotted
myriads of people; they go commonly together.
  Anatomy of Melancholy

**Ben Jonson
1572-1637**

Wine is the milk of Venus
And the poet's horse accounted:
Ply it and you all are mounted.
  Verse over a door at the Devil Tavern

AND HEALTH

**Pamela
Westland**

Mary Queen of Scots bathed in wine but most of
us would be content with cider vinegar, which
has the same effect and restores the acid mantle to
the skin.
  The Encyclopedia of Spices (1979)

Andre Simon	Wine takes over the vitamins contained in the grapes and red wine contains more than white, because red wine is made from juice in which the skins have been left during fermentation.
	Cited by Henry McNulty in 'Your Good Health', *Vogue* (1979)
Edward Whymper fl. 1860s	Wine . . . the only natural remedy (for mountain sickness in the high Andes) . . . most efficacious if taken hot, more especially if a little spice and sugar are added to it.
	Citing Louis Carrel
Andrew Boorde c.1490-1549	Good wine, moderately drunken, doth actuate and doth quicken a man's wits; it doth comfort his heart; it doth scour the liver; it doth engender good blood; it doth comfort and nourish the brain, wherefore it is medicinal . . .
	Dyetary of Helth (1542?)

AND THE INTELLECT

Edward FitzGerald 1809-83	I made a second marriage in my house: Divorced old barren Reason from my bed, And took the Daughter of the Vine to spouse.
	Rubai'yat of Omar Khayyam
Samuel Johnson 1709-84	He said that few people had intellectual resources sufficient to forego the pleasures of wine. They could not otherwise contrive how to fill the interval between dinner and supper.
	Boswell's *Life of Johnson*
W. S. Benwell	There have been many friends with simple tables and modest cellars, about whom it can be said that the soft extractive note of an aged cork being withdrawn has been the true sound of a man opening his heart.
	Journey to Wine in Victoria (1976)

WHAT TO SERVE AND WHEN

H. W. Longfellow 1807-82	When you ask one friend to dine, Give him your best wine! When you ask two, The second best will do!
	Recreations of an Anthologist

| G. K. Chesterton 1874-1936 | And Noah, he often said to his wife When he sat down to dine, 'I don't care where the water goes If it doesn't get into the wine.' *Wine and Water* |

INCLINATION AND RESPONSE

| Ogden Nash 1902-71 | And now I think a glass of wine Would not be too unpleasant, *hein?* *Who'll Buy my Lingual* |

| Benjamin Disraeli 1804-81 | 'I rather like bad wine', said Mr Mountchesney, 'one gets so bored with good wine.' *Sybil* |

| Robert Herrick 1591-1674 | Drink wine, and live here blitheful while ye may; The morrow's life too late, live to-day. *To Youth* |

| Hesiod fl. 735 B.C. | . . . So let me sit in the shade, With a bellyful within me, sipping at my ease The fire-red wine, and turning to face the western breeze. *Works and Days* |

WINE FOR BREAKFAST

Walter James Winston Churchill . . . sometimes pleasantly starts the day with a half bottle of hock . . . Charles Tovay . . . in the eighteen-sixties, recommended claret as an agreeable substitute for tea and coffee at breakfast during warm weather . . . James Denman declared his devotion to a tumbler of light Medoc, diluted with cold water. . .

Antipasto (1957)

WINE WITH WATER

Walter James . . . when diluting wine with water, the water should be put in the glass first. [Denman, explaining that 'most of the fixed air contained in the wine will be fully absorbed by the water, and the mixture will not have that flat or mawkish flavour often recognised if the wine is first placed in the empty glass, by which the aroma is diffused, and a large portion of the more delicate qualities are lost.']

Antipasto (1957)

WINE TASTING AND JUDGING

Andre Launay

There is more rubbish talked about wine and wine tasting than anything else. It is the perfect subject for the snob, the one-up man, the bore . . . and they become more banal as time goes on.

Caviare and After (1964)

Stephen Potter

Don't say too much about wine being 'sound' or 'pleasant': people will think you have been mugging up a wine-merchant's catalogue . . . talk in broken sentences and say 'It has . . . don't you think?'. Or 'It's a little bit cornery'. [It must] pass the test of the *boldly meaningless*.

One-Upmanship (1952)

James Thurber
1894-1961

It's a Naive Domestic Burgundy, Without Any Breeding,
But I Think You'll Be Amused by its Presumption.

Cartoon caption in *Men, Women and Dogs*

Anonymous

To illustrate some of the pompous rubbish written about Australian wines, take this example . . . 'This wine has a ton of quality . . . I drool at the thought of what it will be like with four or five years of bottle age on it'. Drool indeed! What a lot of bloody hooey! . . . I shudder to think of the halucinatory heights this writer would go if he ever had to describe a really good French Chambertin of a good year.

Comment on Len Evans' *Cellarmaster Guide to Australian Wine*, cited by Dan Murphy

Walter James

A young man, invited to a winemen's dinner, invited to give his opinion on one of the wines, held his glass to the light, put it under his nose, surveyed the ceiling with puckered forehead, tasted a little, rolled it once round his mouth, chewed it, consented to swallow, sniffed once more, and finally observed, 'Well, I should call it quite a friendly little wine but — er — scarcely intimate'. Upon which a hard-baked member of the Viticultural Society, sitting alongside asked him, 'Did you really expect it to stand up and embrace you?'

Only the word he used was not "embrace" but something shorter and less delicate!

Wine in Australia (1952)

DISHES AND DINING

AFTERNOON TEA

B. R. Haydon A classic afternoon tea enlivened by Mrs Siddons giving readings from Macbeth. 'After her first reading the men retired to tea. Whilst we were all eating toast ... she began again. It was like the effect of a Mass bell at Madrid: All noise ceased; we slunk to our seats like boors ... with the very toast in their mouths afraid to bite. It was curious to see [Sir Thomas] Lawrence [the portrait painter] in this predicament, to hear him bite by degrees, and then stop for fear of making too much crackle, his eyes full of water from the constraint ...

Cited by Tannahill in *The Fine Art of Food* (1968)

John O'Grady Afternoon teas in Australian homes are for women and teetotallers. You will notice that your host leaves his chair frequently ... He is going out to the garage ... That's where the grog will be.
Aussie Etiket (1971)

BANQUET

Bennett A. Cerf Banquet: a plate of cold, hairy chicken and artificially coloured green peas completely surrounded by dreary speeches and appeals for donations.
Laughing Stock (1945)

BARBECUE

Dom Moraes A distressing Australian habit ... The chance visitor, hospitably invited to grill his own steak ... is first blinded by smoke ... he winds up with a cinder, or with raw meat. But you have to appear to enjoy it: everyone is so anxious to please.

Statement by Indian literary visitor, (1972)

Lynette Wenham

... 'barbecue' is derived from the Spanish word *barbacoa*, meaning 'framework of sticks'. Originally ... used to prepare a whole animal over the fire, to be roasted, grilled or dried.

The Barbecue Cookbook (1978)

BLACK PUDDINGS

David Mabey

Bury puddings come in two types: fatty and dry. The dry ones ... almost entirely composed of blood and oatmeal. The fatty ones with little cubes of pure pork fat set in the pudding mixture ... [at] stalls just outside Bury Market ... stalls sell only black puddings. 'Three hot, please'. The man turns and pulls three steaming puddings from one of the big coppers ... slits each ... and lets the halves open ... hands them over to you ... then reach for the mustard, essential with hot black puddings ... In southern Ireland they make a blood sausage, called 'drisheen', including pig's blood, full-cream milk, breadcrumbs or oatmeal, mace, pepper and a sprig of tansy. In the West Country [of England] an old variation ... A mixture of pig's lights, heart and kidney is cooked, minced and mixed with groats and packed in sausage skins ... and called 'gerty meat puddings'. If pig's blood is added ... they become 'black pots'.

In Search of Food (1978)

BLACKBIRDS

Giovanni de'Rosselli

... you shall put into the Coffin ... as many small live birds as the empty coffin will hold beside the pie aforesaid ... uncovering or cutting up the lid of the Great Pie, all the Birds will fly out, which is to delight and pleasure shew to the company.

Epulario, or *The Italian Banquet* (1598)

Note: The nursery rhyme, 'Sing a Song of Sixpence', can be traced to this source, originally published in Venice in A.D. 1549

Eric Quayle

This was meant to be the *pièce de resistance* of a successful sixteenth-century dinner party ... There seems to have been one obvious snag, that was completely overlooked by the well-meaning compiler of the recipe. Frightened blackbirds (or any other of our feathered friends, from owls to wrens) temporarily enclosed beneath a warm pie-crust are far more likely to leave tangible marks of their extreme displeasure within the dish than display any tendency to burst brightly into song. In fact, a blithely eaten spoonful of the pie's contents after the hasty evacuation of its avian prisoners would dispel the diner's appetite for at least the remainder of that particular meal. One can only wonder if any of the book's more enterprising readers actually tried it out.

Old Cook Books (1978)

BOAR'S HEAD

Anonymous

The noblest dish on the board.
Traditional French saying, cited by Mauduit in *Vicomte in the Kitchen* (1933)

BREAKFAST

P. H. Chavasse
fl. 1870s

A meagre, unsubstantial breakfast causes a sinking sensation of the stomach and bowels. Robert Browning truly remarks that
  'A sinking at the lower abdomen
  Begins the day with indifferent omen.'
'Advice to a Wife', in *Flight of the Duchess*

W. M. Thackeray
1811-63

'No business before breakfast, Glum!' says the King. 'Breakfast first, business next.'
The Rose and the Ring

BAD BREAKFASTS

James Vaux

The breakfast is invariably boiled barley, of the coarsest kind imaginable ... so nauseous that nothing but downright hunger will enable man to eat it.

Life at Sydney Cove for Convicts (1810)

Odgen Nash
1902-71

And you stagger down to break your fast.
Greasy bacon and lacquered eggs
And coffee composed of frigid dregs.

'Traveller's Rest', in *The Face is Familiar*

E. M. Forster
1879-1970

'Porridge or Prunes, sir?' Breakfast had begun. That cry still rings in my memory. It is an epitome — not indeed of English food, but of the forces which drag it into the dirt. It voices the true spirit of gastronomic joylessness. Porridge fills the Englishman up, prunes clear him out ...

'Porridge or Prunes, Sir?'

SUBSTANTIAL BREAKFASTS

Carol Willson and John Goode

Scandinavian breakfasts are ... memorable. The choice of almost everything is by the dozen. Twelve cereals and porridges, a similar number of milks and yoghourts, a dozen types of cheese, cold meats and, of course, a substantial sample collection from the 200 ways of preparing Baltic herring, all to stack into mountains on a choice of breads, rolls or 'biscuits'.

Such quantities seem to be needed by locals in those distant sub-Arctic latitudes, but does the same apply in Germany?

'If It's Herring, This Must be Holland,' *Financial Review* (1985)

Brillat-Savarin
1755-1826

The English and the Dutch eat for their breakfasts bread, butter, fish, ham and eggs, and almost never drink anything but tea.

Physiologie du Goût

Helen Burke

It was Somerset Maugham who said that anyone who came to this country [Britain] from abroad and who wanted three meals a day should order three breakfasts.

Kippers to Caviar (1965)

R. H. Barham
1788-1845

It seems he had taken a light breakfast — bacon,
An egg — with a little boiled haddock — at most
A round and a half of some hot-buttered toast,
With a slice of cold sirloin from yesterday's roast
And then, let me see! He had two — perhaps three
Cups (with sugar and cream) of strong gunpow-
der tea,
With a spoonful in each of some choice *eau de vie*.

The Knight and the Lady

Anthony
Trollope
1815-82

... The tea consumed was the very best, the coffee the very blackest, the cream the very thickest;
there was dry toast and buttered toast, muffins
and crumpets; hot bread and cold bread, white
bread and brown bread, home-made bread and
bakers' bread, wheaten bread and oaten bread ...
there were eggs in napkins, and crispy bits of
bacon under silver covers; there were little fishes
in a little box, and devilled kidneys frizzling on a
hot-water dish ... Over and above this, on a
snow white napkin, spread upon the side-board,
was a huge ham and a huge sirloin; the latter
having laden the dinner table on the previous evening. Such was the ordinary fare at Plumstead
Episcopi.

The Warden

BREAKFAST IN THE USA

Mauduit

Before the Volstead Act brought Prohibition to
America, I was initiated to an original meal — the
Kentucky breakfast ... a bottle of rye whisky, a
pound of steak, and a dog. The dog was there for
the purpose of eating the steak.

Vicomte in the Kitchen (1933)

Rima and
Richard Collin

Eggs Sardou, created at Antoine's (New Orleans)
in 1908 in honor of the visiting French dramatist
Victorien Sardou, was the first of our elaborate

poached-egg dishes. Brennan's Restaurant, founded in 1945, became famous for lavish New Orleans' breakfasts, as popular a feast as dinner at Antoine's.

The New Orleans Cookbook (1979)

Note: Eggs Sardou consists of creamed spinach topped with artichokes, poached eggs and hollandaise sauce — a glorified Eggs Florentine! *J. G.*

BUBBLE AND SQUEAK

Thomas Bridges   [The preamble is] that Neptune, sated with fish, craved meat for his supper . . .

We therefore cook'd him up a dish
Of lean bull-beef with cabbage fried
And a full pot of beer beside;
Bubble they call this dish, and squeak;
Our taylors dine on't thrice a week.

A Burlesque Translation of Homer, cited by Eric Quayle in *Old Cook Books* (1978)

BUSINESS LUNCHES (AND OTHER MEALS)

M. F. K. Fisher (trans.)   An endocrinologist once told me that the best procedure, when business must be combined with eating, is to watch your victim's ear lobes and feed him rare beef. When his lobes turn ruddy, make your proposition . . . and quickly!

Physiology of Taste

Lord Stowell
1745-1836   A dinner lubricates business.

Cited by Philippa Pullar in *Consuming Passions*

CARVING

Eric Quayle   Wynkyn de Worde published *The Boke of Kervynge* in 1508, now in the University Library, Cambridge.

Old Cook Books (1978)

Sydney Smith
1771-1845

In carving a partridge I splashed [Miss Markham] with gravy from head to foot; and I thought I saw three distinct brown rills of animal juice trickling down her cheek, she had the complaisance to swear that not a drop had reached her. Such circumstances are the triumph of civilised life.

Cited by Pullar in *Consuming Passions*

CASSOULET

Anatole France
1844-1924

... a little tavern in the Rue Vavin, Chez Clémence, who makes only one dish, but a stupendous one: *le cassoulet de Castelnaudry* ... Clemence's cassoulet has been cooking for twenty years. She replenishes the pot ... but it is always the same cassoulet. The basis remains, and this ancient and precious substance gives it a taste which one finds in the paintings of old Venetian masters, in the amber flesh-tints of their women.

Histoire comique

Franc-Nohain

Unctuous and perfect, in Languedoc a royal feast, this is called a haricot cream or *cassoulet.*

Nouvelle cuisiniere bourgeoise

CHICKEN MARENGO

R. J. Misch

During the campaign against the Austrians, and after the Battle of Marengo, in 1800, ... all Napoleon's soldiers 'could liberate' for Chef Dunand were three eggs, four tomatoes, six crayfish, a small hen, a little garlic, some oil and a saucepan. Dunand browned the chicken parts in the oil, and fried the eggs in the same oil with a clove or two of garlic, and the tomatoes. He poured over this mixture some water mixed with cognac ... and put the crayfish atop, to cook in the steam. The dish was served in a tin plate, the chicken surrounded by the eggs and crayfish. Napoleon exclaimed: 'Dunand, you must feed me like this after every battle!'

Royal Cookbook (1972)

CHRISTMAS FOODS

**James Scott
(Sgt of Marines)**

Dined off a piece of pork and apple sauce, a piece of Beef and plum pudding, and Crowned the Day with 4 Bottles of Rum, which was the best we veterans could afford.

Diary (Sydney Cove, Australia, 1788)

**John Gay
1688-1732**

But man, curs'd man, on Turkeys preys,
And Christmas shortens all our days;
Sometimes with oysters we combine,
Sometimes assist the savoury chine;
From the low peasants to the lord,
The Turkey smokes on every board.

'The Turkey and the Ant', *Fables*

CORNISH PASTIES

Anonymous

Pastry rolled out like a plate,
Piled with turmut (turnips), tates (potatoes) and
    mate (meat),
Doubled up, and baked like fate
That's a Cornish pasty.

Traditional Cornish description

Note: The true taste comes from the fact that the ingredients are diced (*not* minced), put in raw, and cooked in a slow oven inside the pastry seal. This used to be done every week when I was a child living in Cornwall in the 1940s. Pies of shapes similar to the true ones, but made with mince and cooked fillings are a gross abomination and prostitution of the name. *J. G.*

CURRIES

**Jack Santa-
Maria**

. . . avoid the use of 'curry powders' and get used to making your own . . . The Tamil word *kari* means a sauce or stew . . . the advantage of developing your own . . . is that you will quickly obtain the exact taste which your dishes require . . . It is worth while grinding the spices together from the whole seed, sometimes . . . with garlic, ginger or some other plant.

Indian Meat and Fish Cookery (1977)

Mr [?] Arnot of Greenwich

You may curry anything — old shoes should even be delicious, some old oil cloth or staircarpet not to be found fault with (gloves, if much worn, are too rich).

Cited by Philippa Pullar in *Consuming Passions*

Kenneth Mitchell

Malay curries make great use of the milk of the omnipresent coconut and seldom include yoghurt so favoured by Indian cooks.

A Taste of Malaysia (1980)

DINING

Owen Meredith
1831-91

He may live without love — what is passion but pining?
But where is the man who can live without dining?
Lucile

Lord Byron
1788-1824

All human history attests
That happiness for man — the hungry sinner,
Since Eve ate apples, much depends on dinner!
Don Juan

Joseph Despaze

. . . If you like us not to be witty
And to kill our spirits and transports,
Just put ten women who are pretty
At our table, even mid-course.
. . . Friends, let's stay alone, now as then.
Can our senses lead us astray.
For dinners we'll just keep the men,
And for suppers, the women so gay.

in Grimod de la Reyniere's *Almanach des gourmands*

EXPERIENCES AND IDEALS

Nicolas Boileau-Despréaux
1636-1711

Take fresh heart and never forget that a warmed-up dinner is worth nothing at all.
Le Lutrin

Alexander Pope
1688-1744

The hungry judges soon the sentence sign,
And wretches hang, that jurymen can dine.
Rape of the Lock

Samuel Johnson
1709-84

A man is in general better pleased when he has a good dinner upon his table, than when his wife talks Greek.

Johnsonian Miscellanies

NATIONALITIES AND PERSONALITIES

Oscar Wilde
1854-1900

The man who can dominate a London dinner-table can dominate the world.

Cited by Richard Aldington

E. C. Bentley
1875-1956

Sir Christopher Wren
Said, 'I am going to dine with some men.
If anybody calls
Say I'm designing St Pauls'.

Biography for Beginners

Alphonse Karr
1808-90

Even the great Napoleon could not dine twice.

Le Chemin le plus Court

Lewis Carroll
1832-98

He thought he saw a Banker's Clerk
Descending from the 'bus'
He looked again, and found it was
A Hippopotamus.
'If this should stay to dine', he said,
'There won't be much for us!'

Sylvie and Bruno

Walter James

Gustave Flaubert ... always liked a private dining-room when dining at a restaurant, so that he could take his boots off before attacking the food.

Antipasto (1957)

POST-PRANDIAL REFLECTIONS

Samuel Pepys
1633-1703

Strange to say how a good dinner and feasting reconciles everybody.

Diary

Robert Herrick
1591-1674

'Tis not the food, but the content
That makes the table's merriment.

Content not Cates

H. V. Marrot

From dinners scanty and unwisely blent,
From gastric suppers, nights unwisely spent,
From wines that have not only turned but rent,
Good Lord, deliver us!

'The Litany of Good Companions'

DINNER PARTIES

Thomas Carlyle
1795-1881

If Jesus Christ were to come today, people wouldn't even crucify him. They would ask him to dinner, and hear what he had to say, and make fun of it.

Cited by D. A. Wilson in *Carlyle at his Zenith*

Sydney Smith
1771-1845

An excellent and well-arranged dinner is a most pleasing occurrence, and a great triumph of civilised life. It is not only the descending morsel and the enveloping sauce — but the rank, wealth, wit and beauty which surround the meats . . . in short . . . everything of sensual and intellectual gratification which a great nation glories in producing.

. . . who knows that the kitchen chimney caught fire half an hour before dinner! — and that a poor little wretch, of six or seven years old, was sent up in the midst of the flames to put it out?'

Article to *Edinburgh Review*, cited by Hesketh Pearson in *The Smith of Smiths* (1934)

DISCOVERY AND INVENTION

Brillat-Savarin
1755-1826

The discovery of a new dish does more for the happiness of man than the discovery of a star.

Physiologie du Goût

EATING AND DRINKING

Jonathan Swift
1667-1745

I told him . . . that we ate when we were not hungry and drank without the provocation of thirst.

'Voyage to the Houyhnhms', *Gullivers Travels*

Matthew Prior
1664-1721

Their beer was strong; their wine was port;
Their meal was large; their grace was short.
  An epitaph

Samuel Johnson
1709-84

Nobody can write the life of a man but those who
have eat and drunk and lived in social intercourse
with him.
  Boswell's *Life of Johnson*

ENTERTAINING

Stephen Potter

If you are taking a girl . . . to lunch at a restaurant,
it is WRONG to . . . hold the wine list just out of
sight, look for the second cheapest claret on the
list and say, 'Number 22, please'. . . . Nominate
the wine in English and French, and make at the
same time some comment which shows at least
that you have heard of it before.
  One-Upmanship (1952)

ETIQUETTE

Jules Renard
1864-1910

The truly free man is he who refuses an invitation
to dinner without giving any reason for it.
  Cited in Courtine's *Feasts of a Militant Gastronome*

John Betjeman
1906-85

Phone for the fish-knives, Norman;
As cook is a little unnerved;
You kiddies have crumpled the serviettes
And I must have things daintily served.

Are the requisites all in the toilet?
The frills round the cutlets can wait
Till the girl has replenished the cruets
And switched on the logs in the grate.

It's ever so close to the lounge dear,
But the vestibule's comfy for tea
And Howard is out riding on horseback,
So do come and take some with me.

Now here is the fork for your pastries,
And do use the couch for your feet;
I know what I wanted to ask you —
Is trifle sufficient for sweet?

Milk then just as it comes dear?
I'm afraid the preserve's full of stones;
Beg pardon, I'm soiling the doileys
With afternoon tea-cakes and scones.

How to get on in Society

R. H. Barham
1788-1845

When asked out to dine by a Person of Quality,
Mind, and observe the most strict punctuality!
    For should you come late,
    And make dinner wait,
And the victuals get cold, you'll incur, sure as fate,
The Master's displeasure, the Mistress's hate.
And — though both may, perhaps, be too well
    bred to swear, —
They'll heartily *wish* you — I need not say *Where.*

The Lay of St Cuthbert, or *The Devil's Dinner Party*

Fra Bonvicino

Let thy hands be clean.
Thou must not put either thy fingers into thine
    ears, or thy hands on thy head.
The man who is eating must not be cleaning
By scraping with his fingers at any foul part.

Cited in Tannahill's *Fine Art of Food* (1968)

Bennett Cerf

Good manners: The noise you don't make when
you're eating soup.

Laughing Stock (1945)

Frances Trollope
1780-1863

The frightful manner of feeding with their knives,
till the whole blade seemed to enter into the
mouth; and the still more frightful manner of
cleaning the teeth afterwards with a pocket-knife.

Domestic Manners of the Americans

Jonathan Swift
1667-1745

Fingers were made before forks, and hands before
knives.

Polite Conversation

W. S. Gilbert
1836-1911

The man who bites his bread, or eats peas with a
knife, I look upon as a lost creature.

Ruddigore

FOOD FOR THE GODS

Thomas Hood
1799-1845

There's nectar! There's ambrosium!
The Turtles

S. T. Coleridge
1772-1834

For he on honey-dew hath fed,
And drunk the milk of Paradise.
Kubla Khan

J. G. Whittier
1807-92

To eat the lotus of the Nile
And drink the poppies of Cathay.
The Tent on the Beach

T. B. Aldrich
1839-1907

The pet of the harem, Rose-in-Bloom,
Orders a feast in his favourite room —
Glittering squares of coloured ice,
Sweetened with syrup, tinctured with spice,
Creams, and cordials, and sugared dates,
Syrian apples, Othmanee quinces,
Limes and citrons and apricots,
And wines that are known to Eastern princes.
When the Sultan Goes to Ispahan

**Sir Walter
Ralegh**
c.1552-1618

Eat slowly; only men in rags
    And gluttons old in sin
Mistake themselves for carpet bags
    And tumble victuals in.
Stans Puer ad Mensam

Anonymous

Ladies must decline cheeses and, above all, 'must
not touch the decanters'.
National Encyclopedia of Business and Social Forms
(1882)

E. V. Rieu
fl. mid-20th
century

And so in all propriety they dined upon the beach,
Restricting their consumption to a single helping
    each,
And choosing the right cutlery with cultivated
    ease
For caviare, asparagus, or macaroni cheese.
Pirates on Funafuti

Lord Fisher

Fear less, hope more; eat less, chew more . . .
Records (1919)

Anonymous

1. Do not roll your rice into a ball.
2. Do not gobble your food.
3. Do not swill your soup.
4. Do not eat noisily.
5. Do not crunch bones in your teeth.
6. Do not put back fish and meat you have tasted.
7. Do not throw bones to the dog.
8. Do not snatch.
9. Do not spread your rice out to cool.
10. Do not suck bits of food out of the soup bowl into your mouth.
11. Do not add condiments to the communal soup.
12. Do not pick your teeth.

Book of Etiquette (China, c.1000 B.C.)

Cyrille P. T. Laplace
1793-1875

... the frigid deportment and etiquette of [the English] will not reign long in Australia ... the custom of picnics and parties ... is starting to establish a closer relationship between the sexes, and in consequence, a taste for one another's company, a pleasure of which the English know virtually nothing elsewhere ... Sydney upper-class gentlemen ... behave better towards the fair sex, and do not have the habit, when a meal is ended, of chasing the women from the table so they can spend hours getting drunk.

'On Sydney Manners', *Voyage autour du Monde*, (1831)

FAST FOODS

Derek Cooper

The extension of franchise catering, whereby semi-skilled staff serve food supplied to them from a central depot, means that one gets exactly the same Quikburger in Glasgow that one gets in Oxford Street ... This standardization is not necessarily going to mean that the food will be badly cooked but it will ... have a uniform blandness, what I describe as 'untaste'.

The Bad Food Guide (1967)

| Julia Child | It is the Americans who have managed to crown minced beef as hamburger, and to send it round the world so that even the fussy French have taken to *le boeuf haché, le hambourgaire.* |
| | *Julia Child's Kitchen* (1978) |

| Quentin Crewe | If fast food is so dreadful, one wonders why the rest of the world has seized upon it so eagerly. American ingenuity has devised perfectly palatable ways of eating swiftly-prepared food and we should be grateful for the hamburger, the hot dog, even Kentucky fried chicken, all of which can be pleasant, nutritious and far better than the lugubrious alternative of a sandwich. |
| | *Quentin Crewe's International Pocket Food Guide* (1980) |

FEASTS

| O. W. Holmes 1841-1935 | The true essentials of a feast are only fun and feed. |
| | *Nux Postcoenatica* |

| H. W. Longfellow 1807-82 | Sumptuous was the feast Nokomis Made at Haiwatha's wedding. All the bowls were made of bass-wood, White and polished very smoothly, All the spoons of horns of bison, Black and polished very smoothly . . . First they ate the sturgeon, Nahma, And the pike, the Maskenozha . . . Then on pemican they feasted, Pemican and buffalo marrow, Haunch of deer and hump of bison, Yellow cakes of the Mondamin, And the wild rice of the river. |
| | *Hiawatha's Wedding Feast* |

Robert Courtine	Indeed, terrible meals are often caused by foolish conceit. Thus 'big spreads' become synonymous with far-fetched experiments and bad cooking. Often only courtesy has kept me in my seat when . . .
	. . . thinking, in rage, to hell with this feast, I almost left the table twenty times at least.
	Feasts of a Militant Gastronome (1973)

FISH 'N CHIPS

A. G. Prys-Jones   The face that could have launched a thousand
ships
And burnt the topless towers of Ilium
Is happy, now, to feast on fish and chips
With Harris, prior to the Odeon.
O (Modern) Helen

G. C. Norman   The Spacemen of the Atom Age
On their unearthly trips
Will feed their fissile faces on
Atomic fission chips.
Nuclear Trifle

GOULASH

**E. Mayer-
Browne**   ... an inheritance from ... Hungary. There are
two secrets important to know [in] the making of
every Gulyas:
   (a) that you must use the same weight of
      onions as you use of meat
   (b) that it tastes even better warmed up, and
      the more the merrier
[For] Znaim Gulyas, you add two dill pickles
(cucumbers), cut like a fan for each person. For
more fancy trimmings, use ... fried eggs, ...
hard-boiled egg ... cut-up Frankfurters ... strips
of green or red paprika [capsicums] cooked in the
gravy.
Austrian Cooking for You (1960)

GRACE BEFORE MEALS

**Sir Stephen
Gaselee**   On china blue my lobster red
   Precedes my cutlet brown,
With which my salad green is sped
   By yellow Chablis down.

Lord, if good living be no sin,
   But innocent delight,
O polarise these hues within
   To one eupeptic white!
Grace During Meat (1938)

Charles Lamb
1775-1834

When I have sat at rich men's tables, with the savoury soup and messes steaming up the nostrils and moistening the lips of the guests with desire and a distracted choice, I have felt that the introduction of that ceremony [Grace] to be unreasonable. With the ravenous orgasm upon you, it seems impertinent to interpose a religious sentiment. It is a confusion of purpose to mutter out praises from a mouth that waters.

'Dissertation on Roast Pig', *Essays of Elia*

Jonathan Swift
1667-1745

Does any man of common sense
Think ham and eggs give God offence?
Or that herring has a charm
The Almighty's anger to disarm?
Wrapped in His majesty divine,
D'you think He cares on what we dine?

No Grace Before Meat

Anonymous

Heavenly Father, bless us,
And keep us all alive,
There's ten of us for dinner
And not enough for five.

Hodge's Grace

GUMBO

Rima and Richard Collin

. . . all gumbos are thickened with okra or with filé. In fact it is the okra that gives gumbo its name — *gombo* being an African word for okra . . . The steaming aroma of freshly-caught crabs, shrimp and oysters; the smell of butter and flour browning slowly in a large iron pot over an open fire; the sizzle of freshly-chopped onions, green peppers and 'shallots' added at just the moment the flour and butter turn a rich brown; the scent of chicken and duck slowly cooking into the mixture . . . the taste of fresh okra or exotic sassafras — this adds up to a good Louisiana gumbo.

The New Orleans Cookbook (1979)

HAGGIS

Theodora Fitzgibbon

Haggis is perhaps the best known and most traditional of all Scottish foods. It is eaten at Hogmanay (New Year's Eve) and is often served at banquets and dinners, especially on St Andrew's Day (30 November) and Robert Burns' anniversary (25 January) dinners . . . it is traditional to drink a glass of neat [single-malt] whisky with it, and also to serve it with *Clapshot* [otherwise known as 'tatties and neeps' — potatoes with turnips].

Traditional Scottish Cookery (1980)

George Saintsbury

Generally speaking, Scottish ideas on food are sound. The people who regard haggis . . . as a thing the lips should not allow to enter . . . and the tongue refuse to mention, are, begging their pardon, fools.

A Second Scrapbook

Robert Burns 1759-96

Fair fa'[1] your honest, sonsie[2] face,
Great chieftain o' the puddin' race!
Aboon them a' ye tak your place,
Painch,[3] tripe, or thairm.[4]
Weel are ye wordy o'a grace
As lang's my airm.

Address to a Haggis
[1]Good befall; [2]comely; [3]paunch; [4]intestines

Aristophanes
c.444-380 B.C.

So was I served with a stuffed sheep's paunch I
    broiled
On Jove's day last . . .
Because, forsooth, not dreaming of your thunder,
I never thought to give the rascal vent,
Bounce goes the bag, and covers me all over
With its rich contents of such varied sorts.
    The Clouds

HAMBURGERS

**Ivor H. Evans
(ed.)**

Hamburgers, or **Hamburger steaks**. This
popular American dish of fried minced beef,
onion, egg, etc . . . appears to have originated in
the Baltic region some centuries ago and was
introduced into America in the 19th century by
sailors from Hamburg. The infelicitous beefburger
is an attempt by caterers to avoid confusion by
association with the name of ham.
    Brewer's Dictionary of Phrase and Fable (1977)

Peter Smark

The RAH (Real Aussie Hamburger) peaked as the
quintessence of Australian restaurant food around
1950 . . . The RAH temple was Hamburger Max's
at St Kilda Junction in Melbourne . . . The bun
(stale, absolutely necessary) was toasted . . . on
the same flat grill to drag in more of the same
flavours. Tomato was grilled to sogginess. Lettuce
turning yellow was added. And tomato sauce, always White Crow. The hamburger itself was a
ball of meat removed from the refrigerator with
hands whose honesty was attested by a layer of
black under the nails. Onions were burned black.
The whole, when assembled with soggy, tinned
beetroot, needed a crocodile's mouth to devour. It
didn't drip so much as run. To eat was to be left
with abundant memories, particularly in the area
of the tie.
    'Burger Bliss', *SMH Metro* (1985)

HANGTOWN FRY

Lila Perl

Like most mining towns during the [Californian] gold rush, ... the prices of Hangtown's eateries were hardly in keeping with the squalor without. Hungry miners paid lavishly in gold for ... Hangtown fry — a mess of fried eggs, fried oysters and bacon ... [for] six or seven dollars [in 1851].

Hunter's Stew and Hangtown Fry (1977)

JAMBALAYA

Rita and Richard Collin

On the old Airline Highway, between New Orleans and Baton Rouge, lies a small Spanish Cajun town, Gonzales, the Jambalaya capital of the world ... [It is] a rice dish descended from Spanish *paella* ... seasoned with chilli powder as well as cayenne; one of the secrets ... is the way the hot chicken or sausage fat coats and seals the rice so it keeps its texture during long cooking while absorbing flavours that surround it ...

New Orleans Cookbook (1979)

LUNCHEONS

John Gloag

The table's long and gleaming,
With pads of virgin white,
And the men who are gathered about the board
Are serpentine-fronted and self-assured,
And frequently murmur, 'Quite'!

On a business lunch after a board meeting.

MEALS

Christopher Morley
1890-1957

Philosophy drips gently from his tongue
Who hath three meals a day in guarantee.

So This Is Arden

Robert Courtine

There are two kinds of disastrous meals: those that are naturally bad — because of total incompetence and the [bad] choice of products; and those that are pretentiously bad — because of a desire for far-fetched originality, albeit a desire to do (at least) *something* well.

Feasts of a Militant Gastronome (1973)

MINCE

Edward Lear
1812-88

They dined on mince, and slices of quince
Which they ate with a runcible spoon . . .
'The Owl and the Pussy-Cat'

**'Bon Viveur',
[John and Fanny
Cradock]**

Our family's dismissal of mince from thought and tum is thorough; but then mince is beastly and anyone who has ever had to spend what is euphemistically called a luncheon time in a draughty English country house in winter, pursuing a greasy fringe of mince with a triangle of cold flabby toast will know the worst of English home life and hospitality.

Daily Telegraph Cook's Book (1964)

PARADOX

Louis Golding

A dish of kippers in a studio, a plate of bread and butter in a farmhouse, a pie of peacock's tongues in a flat on Park Avenue, adds itself wildly and lovelily to those supreme gastronomic experiences of a lifetime.

'There Were No Table-napkins' (c.1943)

PARTIES

Elsa Maxwell

Never let the guests do what they want; guests never want to do what *they* want . . . always try to incite some opposition so the conversation sparkles.

Cited by Antonia Williams in *Vogue* (1979)

**Baron James de
Coquet**

There are still hostesses who entertain well . . . they take a little of the best from each era.

Column in *Le Figaro*

Ogden Nash
1902-71

May I join you in the doghouse, Rover?
I wish to retire till the party's over.
  'Children's Party'

William
Wordsworth
1770-1850

Is it a party in a parlour?
Cramm'd just as they on earth were cramm'd —
Some sipping punch, some sipping tea,
But, as you by their faces see,
All silent and all damn'd!
  Unpublished stanza

PICNICS

J. A. Lindon

You are sitting on stones with rheumaticky
  bones,
    and a sandwich with egg in it handed you,
Though the yolk, for a cert, drops a blob on your
  shirt,
    and as non-U the others have branded you; . . .

You are loath to be rude, but you're hating the
  food,
    which is certainly unsatisfying;
Mainly damp-looking lettuce, which felons in
  fetters
    might feed on if very near dying;
There is molten ice-cream, which you do not
  esteem —
    when you're dry there is milk going curdly,
For the tool isn't here that they open the beer
  with, you've left it behind most absurdly;
Then the children get hurt, lie and howl in the
  dirt,
    and you shout at 'em, smack 'em, and shake
    'em,
And you swear that again (*walking* home in the
  rain)
    for a picnic you never will take 'em.
  'The Delights of a Picnic'

Robert
Browning
1812-89

Then I went indoors, brought out a loaf,
Half a cheese, and a bottle of Chablis;
Lay over the grass and forgot the oaf
Over a jolly chapter of Rabelais.
  'Garden Fancies'

| Marie Dressler | If ants are such busy workers, how come they find time to go to all the picnics? |
| | *Cited by Cowan in* The Wit of Women |

PIES

| Eugene Field 1850-95 | But I, when I undress me Each night, upon my knees, Will ask the Lord to bless me With apple pie and cheese. |
| | *Apple Pie and Cheese* |

| Nathaniel Hawkins fl. 19th century | . . . a meat pie, which, if you eat it, weighs upon your conscience, with the idea that you have eaten the scraps of other people's dinners. |
| | *Cited by Philippa Pullar in* Consuming Passions |

| Richard Le Gallienne 1866-1947 | Strange pie that is almost a passion O passion immoral for pie . . . The pie that is marbled and mottled The pie that digests with a sigh For all is not Bass that is bottled And all is not pork that is pie. |
| | 'A Melton Mowbray Pork Pie' |

| Anonymous | Sing a song of sixpence, A pocket full of rye; Four and twenty blackbirds, Baked in a pie. When the pie was opened, The birds began to sing; Wasn't that a dainty dish, To set before the king? |
| | *Note:* How it was done? See *Blackbirds* |

| C. D. Warner 1829-1900 | It is safe almost anywhere to denounce pie, yet nearly everybody eats it . . . snobbish, of course; but snobbery, being an aspiring failing, is some-times the prophecy of better things . . . a line passing through Bellows Falls, and bending a little south, would mark . . . the region of perpetual pie. In this region pie is to be found at all hours and seasons, and at every meal . . . the hill and country |

towns of New England are full of those excellent women . . . who would . . . sink in mortification . . . if visitors should catch them without a pie in the house.

'Pie' in *Backlog Studies* (c.1880)

Pitt the Younger
1754-1806

I think I could eat one of Bellamy's veal pies.

Attrib. last words

AUSTRALIAN MEAT PIES

Anonymous

Whenever a renowned chef or gourmet visits Australia, somebody pushes a meat pie into his hands, sprays it with tomato sauce, demands he takes a bite, and photographs him . . . It is high time there was a Government decree making it . . . punishable by death for anybody to call the meat pie an Australian invention or 'Australia's national dish' . . . It is possible that the meat pie with tomato sauce is a distinctive Australian dish, but why boast about it?

Editorial, *Sydney Morning Herald* (1974)

Phillip Smiles

. . . the woman with the worst job [in Australia] — dropping one pea into every meat pie as it passes her on a production line [and] technically slots the pies into the 'meat and vegetable' variety, to get around the ruling that meat pies contain at least 25 per cent meat . . . some manufacturers were taking the sludge left over from the production of apple juice, mixing it with gelatine and shoving it in pie pastries. One manufacturer said this . . . was for the convenience of customers [who] like to 'drink' the contents . . . without having to chew into bits of apple.

Speech during debate in NSW Parliament, cited in *Sun-Herald* (1985)

PUDDING

Cervantes
1547-1616

The proof of the pudding is in the eating.

Also attributed to Henry Glapthorne in *The Hollander* (1635) and to Addison in *The Spectator*

Joel Barlow
1755-1812

I sing the sweets I know, the charms I feel,
My morning incense, and my evening meal,
The sweets of Hasty Pudding.
  The Hasty Pudding

Ruth Martin

Hasty Pudding:
(i) Simple pudding of boiled milk and sugar, with tapioca, sago, semolina or flour to thicken, served hot with sugar, jam or treacle.
(ii) American dessert of cornmeal, milk and molasses.
  International Dictionary of Food & Cooking (1973)

Charles Dickens
1812-70

Hallo! A great deal of steam! the pudding was out of the copper. A smell like a washing-day! That was the cloth. A smell like an eating house and a pastrycook's next door to each other, with a laundress's next door to that. That was the pudding.
  A Christmas Carol

Susan Ogilvy

Black and white puddings made from animal blood or liver, suet, breadcrumbs and spices, stuffed into intestines and boiled, had been made for many years . . . In Tudor and Stuart times, meatless versions with the addition of cream and eggs were developed, but at first still boiled in intestines. Later the pudding cloth was invented, so that puddings could be made at all times of the year and not only at pig or sheep killing time.
  Curds and Whey (1979)

RED BEANS AND RICE

Anonymous

In all the ancient homes of New Orleans, and in the colleges and convents, where large numbers of children are sent to be reared to be strong and useful . . . several times a week there appear on the table . . . the nicely-cooked dish of red beans, which are eaten with rice.
  The Picayune Creole Cookbook (1900)

Rima and Richard Collin

Louis Armstrong . . . always signed his letters 'Red beans and ricely yours', which expresses perfectly the attachment New Orleanians feel for their favourite dish . . .

The New Orleans Cookbook (1979)

SALADS

Lizzie Boyd

The combination of uncooked, edible leaf vegetables and herbs with dressings was introduced to Britain as early as Roman times . . . the so-called 'Simple Salad' . . . The more complicated 'Grand Salad', which developed later, included a mixture of meat, fish, nuts, raisins, olives, oranges, lemons and other suitable ingredients . . . and came to be known as Salamagundy . . .

British Cookery (1977)

Frank Muir

Salads were for rich people only . . . the only vegetables eaten were cabbages and onions . . .

The Frank Muir Book (1978)

Mortimer Collins
1827-76

O cool in the summer is salad,
And warm in the winter is love . . .
Take endive — like love it is bitter,
Take beet — for like love it is red:
Crisp leaf of the lettuce shall glitter,
And cress from the rivulet's bed:
Anchovies, foam-born, like the lady
Whose beauty has maddened this bard:
And olives, from groves that are shady;
And eggs — boil 'em hard.

'Salad'

Hannah Glasse
1708-70

Take fresh Horse-Dung hot, and lay it in a Tub near the Fire, then sprinkle some Mustard-seeds thick on it, and lay a thin Lay of Horse-Dung over it, cover it close and keep it by the Fire, and it will rise high enough to cut in two Hours.

'To raise a Sallat in two Hours at the Fire', *The Art of Cookery Made Plain and Easy* (1747)

214

Sydney Smith
1771-1845

Two large potatoes, passed through a kitchen
    sieve,
Unwonted softness to the salad give;
Of mordent mustard, add a single spoon,
Distrust the condiment which bites too soon;
But deem it not, thou man of herbs, a fault,
To add a double quantity of salt:
Three times the spoon with oil of Lucca crown,
And once with vinegar, procured from town;
True flavour needs it, and your poet begs
The pounded yellow of two-well boiled eggs;
Let onion atoms lurk within the bowl,
And scarce suspected, animate the whole;
And lastly, on the flavoured compound toss
A magic teaspoon of anchovy sauce:
Then though green turtle fail, though venison's
    tough,
And ham and turkey are not boiled enough,
Serenely full, the Epicure may say —
Fate cannot harm me — I have dined today.

Receipt for Salad given to a Mr Moysey in January,
1843, cited by Hesketh Pearson in *The Smith of Smiths*,
(1934); also in Eliza Acton, *Modern Cookery* (1845)

SANDWICH

Mauduit

Invented by an eighteenth century nobleman . . .
these delicacies, after having degenerated into fix-
tures of the British railways station, have now
become an art . . .

The Vicomte in the Kitchen (1933)

Samuel Johnson
1709-1784

'I like to eat my meat in good company, Sir.'
'So do I, and the best company for meat is bread.
A sandwich is better company than a fool.'

Cited without source by Leyel & Hartley in *The
Gentle Art of Cookery* (1925)

Elna Adlerbert

The open sandwich is of Danish origin, but it has
long been popular all over Scandinavia . . . to do
justice to it you must be generous with the ingredients, so that it is almost a meal in itself. It should
also have visual appeal . . .

Cooking the Scandinavian Way (1961)

SERVING

Edmund Spenser
1552-99

Pour out the wine without restraint or stay,
Pour not by cups, but by the bellyful,
Pour out to all that wull.

Epithalamion

James Boswell
1740-95

The French are an indelicate people ... At Madame du Boccage's ... the footman took the sugar in his fingers and threw it into my coffee. I was going to put it aside, but hearing it was made on purpose for me, I e'en tasted Tom's fingers. The same lady would needs make tea ... The spout of the tea-pot did not pour freely; she bade the footman blow into it. France is worse than Scotland in everything but climate.

Life of Johnson

SHISH-KEBABS

**Georgia
Cheopelas**

Sis (pronounced *shish*) means skewer in Turkish, and 'kebob', from the Arabic *kebap*, means roasted meat. It seems plausible to infer that the first skewer ... was the sword ... The Japanese call it 'kushiyaki'; Moroccans call it 'brochettes'; Spanish — 'pinchos'; South Africans — 'sosaties'; Indonesians — 'sates' ...

Skewer Cooking Around the World (1975)

SMOKED FOODS

Martial
c.43-104

It is not every smoke that is suited to cheese; but the cheese that imbibes the smoke of Velabrum (the popular Roman shopping centre) is excellent.

Cited by Evan Jones in *The World of Cheese* (1976)

**F. Marian
McNeill**

'No sort of meat' says Meg Dods, 'is more improved by smoking with aromatic woods than mutton'.

The Scots Kitchen (1929)

Note: In Australia, 'Scots hams' appear in butchers' shops during the pre-Christmas season. Only legs of local lamb are smoked, as a low-cost alternative to ham, and they are generally available only for about four weeks in the year.

Noel Holmes

I suspect it is often more fun smoking fish than eating them . . . I have smoked fish in a converted outside lavatory (a single-holer) on the Great Barrier, in a converted plywood tea-chest at the Bay of Islands, in a forty-four gallon drum on the Coromandel coast . . . I have yet to meet a fish which quarrels with a smokehouse. Kahawai can be smoked. So can kingfish . . . Roe in season is magnificent . . . the common sprat . . . eels . . . mussels, in fact all shellfish . . . Albert Bowman smokes all the gamefish with the touch of a master — swordfish, sharks and tuna.

Just Cooking Thanks (1976)

SMØRREBRØD

Mette Herborg

. . . *smørrebrød* is to Danes the salt of the earth . . . The Scandinavians are said to be congenitally imperturbable, but when it comes to decorating open sandwiches we prove that we possess both temperament and imagination. Sometimes we overdo it . . . and garnish them with all kinds of trimmings, forgetting that we must not suppress the taste of the main ingredient.

Danish Open Sandwiches (1980)

Carol Willson and John Goode

At Oskar Davidsens [in Copenhagen], going since 1888, the menu is a metre long with *smørrebrøds* ranging from 0.80 cents to $A7 for a shrimp pyramid . . .

'Copenhagen — a Surprising City', *Sun Herald* (1980s)

STEW

R. H. Barham
1788-1845

For, famed as the French always are for ragouts
No creatures can tell what they put in their stews
Whether bull-frogs, old gloves, or old wigs, or old
shoes . . .

'The Bagman's Dog', *Ingoldsby Legends*

Richard Olney ... stews may be said ... to form the philosophical cornerstone of French family cooking ...

Simple French Food (1974)

Edouard de Pomiane The classic *pot-au-feu* is a mixture of beef and vegetables cooked for a long time in salt water.

Cooking with Pomiane (1962)

Lila Perl A 'hunters stew' could contain anything from chunks of bear meat to bits of squirrel ... One common requirement was strong red pepper, to mask the gamey flavour ...

Hunter's Stew and Hangtown Fry (1977)

SUPPER

Thomas Turner Wednesday 22nd ... After ten we went to supper on four boiled chickens, four boiled ducks, minced veal, sausages, cold roast goose, chicken pasty, and ham (about 17 people were present). After, our behaviour ... was downright obstreperous ... dancing or jumping about, without a violin or any musick, singing of foolish healths, and drinking all the time as fast as it could be well poured down ... About three o'clock, finding myself to have as much liquor as would do me good, I slipt away unobserved, leaving my wife to make my excuse.

The Diary of Thomas Turner (a humble grocer from East Hoathly, Sussex, 1754-65)

Robert F. Capon A gentleman should be able to prepare a light supper without removing his jacket.

Angels Must Eat (1969)

Cervantes
1547-1616
In a house where there is plenty, supper is soon cooked.

Don Quixote

Christopher Anstey
1724-1805
If ever I ate a good supper at night,
I dreamed of the devil, and waked in fright.

The New Bath Guide

218

Lord Chesterfield
1694-1773

I am convinced that a light supper, a good night's sleep, and a fine morning, have sometimes made a hero of the same man who, by an indigestion, a restless night, and rainy morning, would have proved a coward.

Letters (1748)

TOAD-IN-THE-HOLE

Susan Ogilvy

Toad-in-the-Hole may be thought to be a very commonplace dish, but in fact the baking of meat, fish and even small birds in a batter or custard pudding goes back to Roman times. Even Hannah Glasse gives a recipe for Pigeons in the Hole . . . rather than the usual sausages.

Curds and Whey (1979)

Philip Harben

The idea behind toad-in-the-hole is that batter is cooked with pieces of meat (often sausages) actually inside it; as the meat cooks, its juices are squeezed into the surrounding batter . . . Following exactly the same technique, excellent toads-in-the-hole can be made with . . . whole sausages (wrapped in bacon for preference).

The Grammar of Cookery (1965)

TRIPE

David Mabey

Tripe . . . was very popular in London about 100 years ago, when it was stewed, curried and even stuffed and roasted on a spit.

In Search of Food (1978)

Gunter Grass
1927-

Who will join me in a dish of tripe? It soothes, appeases the anger of the outraged, stills the fear of death, and reminds us of tripe eaten in former days, when there was always a half-filled pot of it on the stove.

The Flounder

Anne Willan

. . . tripe is baked with onions, carrots and calf's feet, with cider and Calvados, giving the 'Norman flavour' . . . Most French charcuteries sell it in wedges. Tripe used to be the standard pick-me-up at the end of market day ... consumed with dry cider or white wine to balance the richness, then followed by a glass of Calvados. With such sustenance, the homeward path must have seemed short indeed.

French Regional Cooking (1981)

Phileas Gilbert   The origin of [tripe] dishes goes back far into the past. Athenaeus praised this dish ... Homer noted the excellence ... Rabelais tells us how Gargamelle gave birth to Gargantua after having eaten a huge dish of godebillios ... fat tripes ... William the Conqueror enjoyed tripe accompanied by Neustrian apple juice.

La Cuisine (1925), cited in *Larousse Gastronomique*

WELCH RAREBIT

Francis Grose   Welch Rabbit (i.e. a Welch rare-bit): Bread and cheese toasted ... The Welch are said to be so remarkably fond of cheese, that in cases of difficulty their midwives apply a piece of toasted cheese to the *janua vitae* to attract and entice the young Taffy who, on smelling it, makes the most vigorous efforts to come forth.

A Classical Dictionary of the Vulgar Tongue (1788)

David Mabey   There is a world of difference between cheese on toast and Welsh rarebit. The real thing is a mixture of grated cheese, butter, milk or beer, seasoned with salt and pepper and a little mustard, cooked until creamy and spooned over toast. After the mixture has been put under the grill to brown, it is eaten with a glass of beer.

In Search of Food (1978)

SWEETS FOR THE SWEET

BISCUITS

John Fuller Linda, Linda, slender and pretty,
Biscuit girl in a biscuit city,
Packing the biscuits in paper boxes,
What do you dream of? How do you dream?
The cutters rise and fall and rise and cut
The chocolate, the coconut,
The Orange Princess and Gipsy Cream.
The biscuits gather and the boxes shut,
But things are never what they seem . . .
Linda

William . . . his brain —
Shakespeare Which is as dry as the remainder biscuit
1564-1616 After a voyage — he hath strange places crammed
With observations, the which he vents
In mangled forms.
As You Like It

Dylan Thomas Here's your arsenic, dear.
1914-53 And your weedkiller biscuit.
I've throttled your parakeet.
Under Milk Wood

CAKES

Samuel Pepys . . . after a good supper, we had an excellent cake,
1633-1703 where the mark for the Queen was cut . . .
Diaries

Anonymous She whisked the eggs and sugar with a very
solemn air;
The milk and butter also, and she took the
greatest care

To add that little bit of baking powder which
  beginners often omit.
She mixed it all together and she baked it full an
  hour.
But never quite forgave herself for leaving out the
  FLOUR!
The Bride's First Cake

Reay Tannahill   ... the Romans were infinitely fond of
cheesecake ... which may have been a moist
spongy mixture with a texture like cream cheese.
Chrysippus of Tyana in his *Art of making bread*
gave a recipe for a kind of cheesecake made in
Crete ...
The Fine Art of Food (1968)

Anonymous   Pat-a-cake, pat-a-cake, baker's man
Bake me a cake as fast as you can.
Old nursery rhyme

Anonymous   With music and cakes
For to keep up the wakes
Among wenches and fine country beaux.
Old Lancashire song

François Fourier   Instead of by battles and Ecumenical Councils,
1772-1837   the rival portions of humanity will one day dis-
pute each other's excellence in the manufacture of
little cakes.
Cited by Emerson in *Biographical Sketches*

CHOCOLATES

Ogden Nash   If some confectioners were willing
1902-71   To let the shape announce the filling,
We'd encounter fewer assorted chocs,
Bitten into and returned to the box.
Assorted Chocolates

G. Bernard Shaw   What use are cartridges in battle?
1856-1950   I always carry chocolates instead.
Arms and the Man

| Marie de Sévigné 1626-96 | The marquise . . . took too much chocolate, being pregnant . . . that she was brought to bed of a little boy who was black as the devil.
Letters |

CRÊPES SUZETTE

| Stephen Watts | It seems to be impossible to establish dogmatically who invented *crêpes Suzette* . . . One of the most popular stories is that Escoffier created the dish especially for Edward VII (then Prince of Wales). The Prince asked what it was and Escoffier said it had no name yet. He asked the Prince for a suggestion and, it is said, the Prince named it after his dinner companion . . . the same story has also been attributed to . . . Charpentier.
The Ritz (1963) |

CUSTARD

| Ambrose Bierce 1842-c.1914 | Custard: A detestable substance produced by a malevolent conspiracy of a hen, the cow and the cook.
The Enlarged Devil's Dictionary |

| Jane Austen 1775-1817 | I do not advise the custard.
Emma |

DESSERTS

| J. C. Jeafferson | Dessert (from Latin *deservire*): a new word for the 'after course' of superfluous delicacies *served* on removal of the last of the services.
Citing Skinner, philologist (d.1667), in *A Book about the Table* (1875) |

| Oswald Burdett | Dessert: a word covering *both* dishes (cheese and fruit) that came into use in the seventeenth century.
A Little Book of Cheese (1935) |

P. B. Shelley
1792-1822

Though we eat little flesh and drink no wine,
Yet let's be merry: we'll have tea and toast;
Custards for supper, and an endless host
Of syllabubs and jellies and mince pies,
And other such lady-like luxuries.

    Letter to Maria Gisborne

Horace Walpole
1717-97

Our sweets for a long time imitated Nature. But to the ... candy sugared cottages and temples, have succeeded more virile ways of ending our meals. Gigantic figures have taken the place of pigmies and we know that a famous chef, Lord Albermarle's ... complained because his Lordship would not give permission for the demolition of the dining room ceiling to facilitate entry [of a set piece eighteen feet high].

    Cited by X. M. Boulestin in *Ease and Endurance* (1948)

FRITTERS

Mr W. M.

To Make Fritters: Take half a pint of Sack, a pint of Ale, some Ale yeast, nine Eggs, yolks and whites; beat them very well, the eggs first, then altogether, put in some Ginger, and salt, and fine flower [flour], then let it stand an hour or two, then shred in the Apples when you are ready to fry them; your suet must be Beefe suet, or halfe Beefe and half Hogges suet, tryed out of the lease.

    The Queen's Closet Opened (1655)

Alexandre Dumas
1802-70

The name *beignet* (fritter) comes from a Celtic word meaning swelling or tumor ... a sort of dough, fried in a pan, which usually encloses a slice of some sort of fruit.

    Dumas on Food, trans. A. and J. Davidson (1979)

HONEY

Rupert Brooke
1887-1915

And is there honey still for tea?
    The Old Vicarage, Grantchester

A. A. Milne	Isn't it funny
1882-1956	How a bear likes honey?
	Buzz! Buzz! Buzz!
	I wonder why he does?

Winnie-the-Pooh

Arthur	While Honey lies in Every Flower, no doubt,
Guiterman	It takes a Bee to get the Honey out.
1871-1943	*A Poet's Proverbs*

Anonymous

Within this hive,
We're all alive,
Good liquor makes us funny,
So if you're dry,
Come in and try
The Flavour of our honey.

Inn sign of 'The Beehive' at Abingdon, Berkshire,
cited in Silcock's *Verse and Worse* (1952)

ICE-CREAM

| **Wallace Stevens** | The only emperor is the emperor of ice cream. |
| 1879-1955 | *The Emperor of Ice Cream* |

Susan Ogilvy

Iced sweets are reputed to have been made . . . as far back as 3000 B.C. by the Chinese . . . [it was] not until the thirteenth . . . century AD that the recipes were brought to Italy . . . and in Britain appeared in the eighteenth century. Early ice-creams were made in special pewter containers, an inner bowl for the cream and an outer one for the mixture of broken ice and salt . . .

Curds and Whey (1979)

MARMALADE

Anonymous

Oxford gave the world marmalade and a manner.

Paul Jennings

When numbered pieces of toast and marmalade were dropped on various samples of carpet, arranged in quality from coir matting to the finest

Kirman rugs, the marmalade downwards incidence . . . varied indirectly with the quality of the carpet . . . the Principle of the Graduated Hostility of Things.

Even Oddlier

PANCAKES

Mauduit

. . . should be as light as feathers, as thin as tissue paper, and the rim should be crisp while the centre should be very soft.

The Vicomte in the Kitchen (1933)

Anonymous

On Tuesday Shrove there sounds a bell;
To passers-by it rings to tell
Prepare to eat your Pancake.

Old London street cry

'Bon Viveur'
[John and Fanny
Cradock]

Chefs . . . make them in advance, and turn them out on to squares of oiled, greaseproof paper . . . these are thin pancakes, not those wash-leather jobs that look fine for polishing car windows . . . Please say to yourself, 'If a pancake is thick enough to toss, there is only one place to toss it — *into the dustbin.*

The Daily Telegraph Cook's Book (1964)

PRESERVES

Lewis Carroll
1832-98

The rule is, jam to-morrow and jam yesterday — but never jam today.

Through the Looking Glass

Epicurus
c.342-270 B.C.

The blood-red fruitage of a summer's day,
The Autumn orchard's gold and purple spoil,
Gleam here, encrystalled by the tropic cane.

Cited by Mauduit in *The Vicomte in the Kitchen*

REFRESHMENTS

C. J. Dennis
1876-1938

Then Juliet wakes up an' sees 'im there,
Turns on the water-works an' tears 'er 'air,
'Dear love,' she sez, 'I cannot live alone!'
An' wiv a moan,
She grabs 'is pockit knife, an' ends 'er cares . . .
'Peanut or lollies!' sez a boy upstairs.
'The Play', *The Sentimental Bloke*

W. S. Gilbert
1836-1911

I accept refreshments from any hands, however
lowly.
The Mikado

SACHERTORTE

E. Mayer-Browne

Prince Metternich . . . once said to Mr Sacher . . .
of the well-known hotel: ' — Why don't you
make a plainer and more masculine gateau? All
these rich cream creations are only for sweet-
toothed women.' So Mr Sacher made up the
recipe.
Austrian Cooking for You (1960)

Note: Publication of this recipe in Vienna effectively
does away with those claims that the recipe is a 'trade
secret', and impossible to duplicate.

SUGAR

Sydney Smith
1771-1845

A dreadful controversy has broken out in Bath,
whether tea is most effectually sweetened by
lump or pounded sugar; and the worst passions of
the human mind are called into action by the
pulverists and the lumpists. I have been pressed
by ladies on both sides to speak in favour of their
respective theories, at the Royal Institution . . .
Letter to Lady Holland, cited by Hesketh Pearson in
The Smith of Smiths (1984)

SWEETNESS AND SWEETENERS

Henry Fielding
1707-54

Love and scandal are the best sweeteners of tea.
Love in Several Masques

Charles Lamb
1775-1834

To pile honey upon sugar, and sugar upon honey, to an interminable tedious sweetness.
'A Chapter on Ears', *Essays of Elia*

SYLLABUB

Walter James

The elegant Horace Walpole of Strawberry Hill ... once concluded an elaborate ... luncheon party by taking his guests out to the garden and regaling them with ... syllabub. Some sweet wine was poured into tumblers, which were held under the teats of a herd of cows and filled, by pretty dairymaids, with milk warm and foaming direct from its source.
Antipasto (1957)

Susan Ogilvy

The name 'syllabub' derives from the old French champagne 'Sille' and the word 'bub' which was common Elizabethan slang for a bubbling drink; the wine ... was mixed with frothing cream to make a Sille Bub ... the most simple was one in which milk ... was milked directly into a bowl of sweetened and spiced cider, wine or beer ... sometimes known as 'Hatted Kit' ... dairies were turned into elegant rooms, where rich country ladies took their friends to drink syllabubs warm from the cow.
Curds and Whey (1979)

TARTS

Lewis Carroll
1832-98

The Queen of Hearts, she made some tarts
All on a summer's day;
The Knave of Hearts, he stole those tarts,
And took them quite away!
Alice in Wonderland

| Rosemary Wadey | . . . open tarts date back a long time but became very popular in the seventeenth century, when all manner of fillings were used, both sweet and savoury . . . |
| | *Baking Country Breads and Pastries* (1980) |

| Hanna Wolley fl. mid-late 17th century | Tafety-Tart stemmed from the notion that the iced crust of this pie had the sheen of a piece of taffeta cloth. The relevant part of the recipe read, 'then ice them with Rosewater, Sugar, and Butter beaten together, and wash them over with the same, strew more fine sugar over them, and put into the oven again; this done, you may serve them hot or cold.' |
| | *The Gentlewoman's Companion* (1673) |

| 'Bon Viveur' [John and Fanny Cradock] | The popularity of . . . tarts in Britain is very great but a vast number of them are dreadful. Most . . . seem to be closely related to village ponds. Bits of fruit-flotsam drift about in quantities of murky water . . . The final dreadful pall of ersatz custard . . . strewn over it like yellow glue . . . |
| | *The Daily Telegraph Cook's Book* (1964) |

ZUPPA INGLESE

| Quentin Crewe | . . . kind of trifle with sponge cake (often suspiciously bright red), cream and liqueur. |
| | *Quentin Crewe's International Pocket Food Book* (1980) |

| Elizabeth David | . . . that exuberant joke, the *Zuppa Inglese*, a Trifle much glorified, it is true, but still a Trifle. |
| | *Italian Food* (1954) |

OTHER LIQUORS AND THEIR USE

ABSINTH

Addison Mizner
1876-1933

Absinth makes the heart grow fonder.
The Cynics Calendar

Charles H. Baker Jr

It will come as no world-shattering scoop to our readers to hear that people have believed that . . . of late, Absinthe . . . affords certain amiable aphrodisian attributes. All this wishful thinking . . .
The South American Gentleman's Drinking Companion (1951)

Jack Hibberd

Absinth makes the parts go stronger . . .
Odyssey of a Prostitute (1983)

AKVAVIT

Alexis Lichine

A spirit, found generally in the Scandinavian countries, distilled from grain or rectified potato spirit and flavoured with . . . caraway seeds in particular . . . drunk chilled . . . a contraction of the Latin *aqua vitae* meaning water of life.
Encyclopedia of Wines and Spirits (1975)

Cyril Ray

(There are some too, and especially in Denmark, who refer to akvavit as 'snaps' or 'schnapps') . . . the bottle must be cold enough to be frosty with dew, the glass should be small enough to make it impossible for the dram to get lukewarm before it is finished . . . a very potent drink . . . taken with a strong, salty herring.
The Complete Book of Spirits and Liqueurs (1977)

Nika Hazelton

. . . All Danish akvavit is made in Aalbord . . . with an alcoholic strength of 86 per cent proof. You eat a bite and follow with a sip, or if you're strong or Danish, with a full glass of akvavit. This, in turn, is followed immediately with a beer chaser.

Danish Cooking (1967)

Anonymous
Pure as a maiden's heart and strong as her lover;
Hot as the heart so ardently lit;
Cool as the well where spring breezes hover.
That — that, my friend, is *en dansk akvavit*.

Verse on a *kluksflaske* (special decanter) that says *kluk-kluk* as you pour

ALCOHOLIC BEVERAGES

Richard Batt
A research team in New Zealand has claimed that alcohol is less toxic than meat and sugar and less damaging to health than butter, and that a couple of drinks a day could help prevent heart disease ... the human body is superbly equipped to handle moderate amounts of alcohol.

Report from Director of Alcohol Research, Massey University, cited in *Sydney Morning Herald*, 11 April 1984

BITTERS

Walter James
Angostura ... is good in all manner of soups and sauces (especially apple sauce) ... [it goes] well, too, with prunes and rhubarb if you find pleasure in those sorts of things.

Antipasto (1957)

Charles H. Baker Jr
[bitters] are absolutely essential to the creation of scores and scores of the world's best mixed drinks: drinks which without such aromatic pointing-up would be short-lived, spineless and ineffectual things.

The Gentleman's Companion (1946)

CIDER

Elizabeth David   Cider is not merely a substitute for white wine in cooking; the flavour it imparts to fish is excellent and original.

Italian Food (1979)

Christopher Morley
1890-1957

What makes the cider blow its cork
With such a merry din?
What makes those little bubbles rise
And dance like harlequin?
It is the fatal apple, boys,
The fruit of human sin.

A Glee Upon Cider

David Mabey   ... 'cider' derives from the Latin *sicera*, meaning 'strong drink'. And your first taste of true cider, the 'scrumpy' made in a few farmhouses ... can be devastating ... Cider making was introduced from France in the 12th century ... the apples themselves were nothing like the ones we pick today. They were crab ... apples planted in hedgerows ... the cider they yielded was very strong, smoothed with honey and often spiced.

In Search of Food (1978)

COCKTAILS

George Ade
1866-1944

The cocktail is a pleasant drink,
It's mild and harmless, I don't think.
When you've had one, you call for two,
And then you don't care what you do.
Last night I hoisted twenty-three
Of these arrangements into me;
My wealth increased, I swelled with pride;
I was pickled, primed and ossified.

'REMORSE', *The Sultan of Sulu*

Prince de Viggiano

A true mixologist is something of a chemist and a psychologist. He must develop some of the qualities of a chameleon, yet retain a personality of his own.

Foreword to *The Artistry of Mixing Drinks* by Frank Meier (1936)

Burton Stevenson	Napoleon I is said to have invented a cocktail. His favourite pick-me-up was called a 'Rose'.

Stevenson's Book of Quotations (1935)

CRÈME DE CACAO

Raymond Postgate	Put a blob of cream in it and at seventeen she'll find it divine.

'A Table of Liqueurs', *Lilliput* (1954)

DRINKING

WHY DRINK?

Henry Aldrich
1647-1710

If all be true that I do think
There are five reasons we should drink:
Good wine, a friend, or being dry,
Or lest we should be, bye and bye,
Or any other reason why.

Translation of 16th century Latin epigram of Père Sirmond (published in Menage's *Menagiana*), in Playford's *Banquet of Music* (1689)

Anonymous

All animals are strictly dry,
They sinless live and swiftly die.
But sinful, Ginfull, Rum-soaked men
Survive by three-score years and ten,
And some of us — a Mighty Few —
Keep drinking 'till we're 92.

Rhyme printed on a tea-towel

William Congreve
1670-1729

To drink is a Christian diversion
Unknown to the Turk or the Persian.

The Way of the World

Edward FitzGerald
1809-83

Drink! for you know not whence you came, nor why!;
Drink! for you know not why you go, nor where.

Rubai'yat of Omar Khayyam

Oliver Goldsmith
1728-74

Let schoolmasters puzzle their brain,
With grammar, and nonsense, and learning;
Good liquor, I stoutly maintain,
Gives *genius* better discerning.
    She Stoops to Conquer

S. T. Coleridge
1772-1834

Some men are like musical glasses — to produce
their finest tones you must keep them wet.
    Table Talk

Henry Lawson
1867-1922

Drink . . . is stronger than unionism.
    'The Union Buries Its Dead'

WHEN TO DRINK?

H. L. Mencken
1880-1956

I've made it a rule never to drink by daylight and
never to refuse a drink after dark.
    New York Post

WHERE TO DRINK AND THE SERVICE

G. K. Chesterton
1874-1936

I rose politely in the club
And said 'I feel a little bored
Will someone take me to the pub . . .'
    Ballade of an Anti-Puritan

Anonymous

Come where the booze is cheaper,
Come where the pots hold more;
Come where the boss is a bit of a joss,
Come to the pub next door.
    Victorian music-hall song

WHAT TO DRINK?

Samuel Johnson
1709-84

Claret is the liquor for boys; port for men; but he
who aspires to be a hero . . . must drink brandy.
    Boswell's *Life of Johnson*

W. Bridges-Adams

You, Mister Belloc, thought it fine
To put one's faith in God and Wine;
You see the pickle I am in,
Who put my faith in Men and Gin.
    Reproach (c.1950s)

G. K. Chesterton
1874-1936

You will find me drinking rum
Like a sailor in a slum,
You will find me drinking beer like a Bavarian,
You will find me drinking gin
In the lowest kind of inn
Because I am a rigid vegetarian.

So I cleared the inn of wine,
And I tried to climb the sign . . .
The Logical Vegetarian

Thomas Adams
fl. 1612-53

Those bottled windy drinks that laugh in a man's
face and then cut his throat.
Works

Thomas Moore
1779-1852

If with water you full up your glasses,
You'll never write anything wise
For wine is the horse of Parnassus,
Which hurries a bard to the skies.
Anacreontic

HOW TO DRINK

François
Rabelais
c.1494-1553

I do not drink more than a sponge.
Works

John Fletcher
1579-1625

Come landlord, fill a flowing bowl
Until it does run over,
Tonight we will all merry be —
Tomorrow we'll get sober.
The Bloody Brother

James Shirley
1596-1666

I can drink like a fish.
Works

Frank Meier

The art of rational drinking is an accomplishment
as indispensable as dancing or bridge, and a fair
knowledge of wines and liqueurs, their prov-
enance, characteristics, best years, etc., forms part
of a gentleman's culture ... To know how to
drink is as essential as to know how to swim, and
one should be at home in both these closely re-
lated elements. Each man reacts differently to alcohol; he should know before the time when,

according to custom, he indulges in his first collegiate 'binge', whether liquor affects his head, his legs or his morals; whether he sings, fights, weeps, climbs lamp-posts or behaves with excessive affection towards the opposite sex; whether, in short, it makes him a jovial companion or a social pest. *In vino veritas* does not mean that a man will tell the truth when in drink, but he will reveal the hidden side of his character.

Cited by Stephen Watts in *The Ritz* (1963)

ITS EFFECTS

William Shakespeare 1564-1616

Drink provokes the desire, but it takes away the performance.
Macbeth

Anonymous

At the first cup, man drinks wine;
At the second cup, wine drinks wine;
At the third cup, wine drinks man.
Japanese proverb

Beaumarchais 1732-99

Drinking when we are not thirsty and making love all the year round, madam; that is all there is to distinguish us from the other animals.
Le Barbier de Seville

ADVICE

Anonymous

Beer on cider
Is a very bad rider!
A 'wise saw' from Gloucestershire

Anonymous

At a North Queensland motel the dining room was not licensed. 'Think nothing of it', said the waitress. 'If you want a bottle of beer with your steak, just say 'Steak and laundry'. It doesn't show in the records'.
Sydney Morning Herald (1970s)

Eric Parrott

Remember, then, a maiden oughter
Shun all drink and stick to woughter.
Advice to a Young Lady on the Subject of Alcohol (n.d.)

New Testament	Drink no longer water, but use a little wine for thy stomach's sake and thine often infirmities. *Timothy*
George Herbert 1593-1633	Drink not the third glass — which thou can'st not tame When once it is within thee. *The Church Porch*
Rochester 1647-80	Cupid and Bacchus my saints are; May Drink and Love still reign. With Wine I wash away my Cares And then to Love again . . . Cited by Nancy Quennell in *The Epicure's Anthology*

TOASTING

Anonymous	Here's to the girl who lives on the hill, She won't but her mother will. Here's to her mother!!! Traditional RAF toast, late 1940s
Anonymous	There's one long toast that the drover drinks Whether fleece he drives, or hide, And the toast he gives, as the glass he clinks, Is the good dog at his side . . . So a health to the dog, and one to the pup (He sleeps in the trap just now). Not a heel-tap, my lad, tip your glass right up, To the drover's pal — Here's how . . . 'The Drover's Toast', *Bulletin* (19th century)
Jerome K. **Jerome** 1859-1927	. . . we never *eat* anybody's health, always *drink* it. Why should we not stand up now and then and eat a tart to somebody's success? 'On Eating and Drinking', *Idle Thoughts of an Idle Fellow*

GIN

William Bolitho 1890-1930	The shortest way out of Manchester is notoriously a bottle of Gordon's gin. *Twelve Against the Gods: Cagliostro (and Seraphina)*

Michael Green   Gin is a good cure for constipation.
The Art of Coarse Drinking (1973)

Walter James   The fishermen of Cornwall . . . were much given
to a drink they called Mahogany. It was a simple
mixture of two parts gin and one part treacle, well
beaten together.
Antipasto (1957)

John Masefield   Meanwhile, my friend, 'twould be no sin
1878-1967   To mix more water with your gin.
We're neither saints nor Philip Sidneys,
But mortal men with mortal kidneys.
The Everlasting Mercy

Charles H. Baker   Senora Baker Gin Bride-on-the-Rocks came liter-
Jr.   ally out of the wide blue Andean yonder . . . two
miles above the sea . . . There is, insofar as our
wide experience calls, no drink at all like it. It is
drier than a camel's tonsils, blessed with simplicity, virginally cool to view, has a lovely flower
bouquet and bites you like a kind cobra.
The South American Gentleman's Companion (1951)

GRAND MARNIER

Stephen Watts   . . . Marnier Lapostolle, a wealthy owner of vineyards, had once brought to Ritz a liqueur he had
invented. Ritz tasted it and approved. Lapostolle
decided to put it on the market, but he needed a
name for it. Lapostolle was a little man, inclined
to pomposity. Ritz said, half-ironically, 'Why not
call it Le Grand Marnier?' Lapostolle did, and
made a fortune.
The Ritz (1963)

ICE IN DRINKS

Eugene Field   How gracious those dews of solace
1850-95   that over my senses fall,
At the clink of the ice in the pitcher
the boy brings up the hall.
'The Clink of Ice'

Charles H. Baker Jr ... one ice shaver or very fine crusher for juleps ... A heavy canvas bag and wood mallet is as good as any. If getting one of those gadgets which grind up ice cubes finely, don't try to beat the game by getting one for 70 cents ... get one big enough to hold more than one cube at a time, and conserve sanity.

'Miscellaneous Bar Equipment', *The Gentleman's Companion: An Exotic Drinking Book* (1946)

LIQUOR

George Saintsbury There is absolutely no scientific proof of a trustworthy kind that moderate consumption of sound alcoholic liquor does a healthy body any harm at all.

Notes on a Cellar-Book (1920)

William Shakespeare 1564-1616 Though I look old, yet I am strong and lusty;
For in my youth I never did apply
Hot and rebellious liquors to my blood.
As You Like It

Ogden Nash 1902-71 Candy
Is dandy
But liquor
Is quicker.
'Reflections on Ice-Breaking', *The Face is Familiar*

G. W. Young fl. 1900 Though in silence, with blighted affection, I pine,
Yet the lips that touch liquor must never touch mine.
'The Lips that Touch Liquor'

MEAD

Palladius fl. 1420 For mead: at the rising of the dog-star, add a pint of skimmed honey to six of clear water. In boilers, let naked children shake it five hours to and fro, vessel and all. Afterwards, in the sun, with forty days' standing it is done.

On Husbandrie, ed. Rev. Barton Lodge (1873, 1879)

Laurens van der Post

In Ethiopia ... the young boy then presented us all with earthenware drinking vessels ... they did not make the liquid they contained more evocative than it was to me on this occasion. It was my first taste of *tedj*, the mead of ancient Britons and hydromel of the Greeks ... It was a refined and highly civilised liquid with the sparkle of a golden hock.

First Catch Your Eland (1977)

John Goode

I remember my introduction to Australian mead. It was a stinkingly hot day in late summer and, during a visit to McLaren Vale (South Australia), we called at Daringa Cellars, which were without air conditioning. Ken Maxwell, the winemaker, *insisted* we sample his meads 'as they should be drunk' — in winter! While we were fanning ourselves, he disappeared ... Some minutes later, he returned with his own version of mulled mead ... As we discovered some months later, it is a divine refreshment to welcome anyone in from a bitter winter's night.

'Hot Helpers', *Vogue Living* (1981)

PUNCHES — HOT AND COLD

Alexis Soyer
1809-58

But we cannot pass in silence the memorable punch given in 1746 by Sir Edward Russell ... the bowl was the marble basin of a delightful garden ... filled with four large barrels of brandy, eight barrels of filtered water, 25,000 citrons, 80 pints [48 litres] of lemon juice, 13 hundredweight [662kg] sugar, five pounds [2.27kg] nutmeg, 300 biscuits and a pipe of Malaga wine. An awning over the basin protected it from rain which might have disturbed the chemical combination of the delicious beverage ... to serve the joyous company, which numbered more than 6000 persons.

The Pantropheon (1854)

John Goode

When Charles H. Baker Jr ... decided to compile his drinking records of a lifetime, he coined the term 'Hot Helpers' ... the need for people with discrimination to have something which would transform a blue-tipped nose caused by a freezing winter's night into a proboscis of more convivial hue. A Hot Helper must be strong, potent, pungent and just below boiling point. It must have the seductiveness of a siren, the smoothness of velvet and the hidden kick of a Brahmin bull. It must be the perfect counter to the bracing Antarctic 'breezes' in mid-winter Melbourne or Hobart.

'Hot Helpers', *Vogue Living* (1981)

RUM

Bill Scott

Bundaberg rum, overproof rum,
will tan your insides, and grow hair on your bum.
Let the blue-ribbon beat on his empty old drum
or his water-logged belly, we'll stick to our rum.

'Bundaberg Rum', *Songs of the Great Australian Balladists* (1978)

George Mackanness

The population of Sydney in 1806 was divided into two classes. Those who sold rum and those who drank it.

The Life of Vice-Admiral William Bligh

TEQUILA

Charles H. Baker Jr

Tequila is the . . . distilled fermented juice of the *Zotol Maguey* plant . . . and has a strange exotic flavour, which . . . is an acquired taste.

The Gentleman's Companion II (1946)

Cyril Ray

Tequila is said to be the drink of the Mexican middle classes, whereas mescal — which has traces of the hallucinatory drug, mescaline, in it — is the peon's tipple. . . . a ritualistic way of taking [Tequila] is after a suck at a slice of lemon and lick of a pinch of salt . . . Whether it is worth the trouble is a matter for debate . . .

The Complete Book of Spirits and Liqueurs (1977)

COOK'S TOUR

AUSTRALIAN FOOD

Anonymous

Australia is not noted for its native cuisine. Asked to nominate Australia's national dish, we would generally be at a loss. We have developed no distinctive style of cooking like the Chinese, nor established a tradition of fine foods — like the French or Italians. A roast leg of mutton is probably fairly Australian, but our neighbours across the Tasman [New Zealanders] claim their Canterbury lamb is superior to anything grown here.

Our gifts to the gastronomic world are slight. The lamington is an interesting cake for afternoon tea in Alice Springs but it is hardly in the class of some Danish pastries. The mighty pavlova, dripping with passionfruit and topped with mountainous swirls of crusted meringue, may set tastebuds of Australian youth watering, but it has never had the gourmets of Paris besieging the doors of the Australian embassy, begging for the recipe.

'A slippery debate', *Weekend Australian* (1985)

Francis Lancelott

On Monday we've mutton, with damper and tea;
On Tuesdays, tea, damper and mutton,
Such dishes I'm certain all men must agree
Are fit for peer, peasant and glutton.
'On Monday We've Mutton' (c. 1852)

Traditional

Fair Australia. Oh what a dump.
All you get to eat is crocodile,
Bandicoot's brains and catfish pie.
Let me go home again before I die.
Cited in *The Ugly Australian* (1976)

George Meudell
1860-1936

How few Australians know anything about wines, and how very few drink anything regularly but vile, filthy whisky and gaseous, unwholesome beer.

The Pleasant Career of a Spendthrift (1929)

Geoffrey Blainey [Europeans] often concluded that the land was mean and hungry, not realizing that some regions*, in the course of four seasons, provided a wider variety of foodstuffs than a gourmet in Paris would eat in an extravagant year.

Triumph of the Nomads (1975)
* This should really read 'in some years, in some places'.

Richard Twopeny 1857-1915 Of course meat is the staple of Australian life. A working-man whose family did not eat meat three times a day would indeed be a phenomenon. High and low, rich and poor, all eat meat to an incredible extent, even in the hottest weather.

Town Life in Australia (1883)

Bill Olson . . . the Greek café [in Australia] open all day and all night. Steak cut from drovers' old boots, limp shredded lettuce, one tomato slice, bitumen-black tea from a pot wadded with generations of sour leaves. Banana special, fruit salad and ice-cream, peach Melba.

National Times (1975)

Carol Willson, John Goode and Liz Kaydos Still more [Greeks] appreciated the need for reasonable food to be available for travellers and locals in country towns. It has justifiably been claimed that outback Australia was fed for eighty years by Greeks. They established cafes in many country towns. Some men bought hotels . . . by doing this they performed an invaluable service . . .

Greek-Australian Cookbook (1982)

BRITISH COLONIAL CUISINE

Agnes Keith I was slow at first about learning the Sandakan [North Borneo] food regulations. I used to eat lamb without peas, roast beef without Yorkshire pudding, eggs without bacon, toast without marmalade, and I would contract without shudder the mixed marriage of vegetables and fruit. I know the proper combinations now, and no longer baste mutton with mustard or use Worcester sauce with scrambled eggs ... But on my return to America, I shall go and sit by the service door of a restaurant and watch ... while sausages mate with sauerkraut and baked beans furnish a meal and a half, where ice-cream is a labour of love and lettuce have hearts and aren't ashamed to show them.

Land Below the Wind (1939)

BRITISH COOKING

Marika Hanbury Tenison
British cooking owes a lot to ... breakfast and high tea.

The Best of British Cooking (1976)

CARIBBEAN FOOD

Connie and Arnold Krochmal
The most authentic Caribbean appetiser is a spread known as gundy, usually a mixture of seafood, onions, peppers, olives, and other vegetables and seasonings.

Caribbean Cooking (1974)

CHINESE TOUCH

Curnonsky
1872-?
France and China are the only two countries that have both cuisine and courtesy.

Cited in *Feasts of a Militant Gastronome* (1973)

Hilaire Belloc
1870-1953
Birds in their little nests agree
With Chinamen, but not with me; ...

On Food

Ch'u Yuan
Roasted Daw, steamed widgeon and grilled quail —
On every fowl they fare.

Boiled perch and sparrow broth — in each
preserved
The separate flavour that is most its own.
The Great Summons (3rd century B.C.)

Tu Fu
They are at ease in the Inner Court,
With ivory sticks, gold-tipped,
Pick at the fish on a crystal plate, at camel hump.
When bored, they drink.
In endless courses serve the Royal Table,
With foods like loops and skeins entangled,
Eunuchs stand at the palace gate;
Piebald horses, reined, fret and wait.
Parade of Beauties (c. A.D. 740)

John Goode
To eat in a Chinese restaurant, four is really the
minimum number and six or eight are preferable.
You should order one dish for each person, plus
one more, as well as soup. Fruit is often served at
the end as a palate freshener.
Twenty Great Meat Dishes in Taiwan (1984)

Kenneth Lo
The general change suffered by Chinese food
when it goes abroad can be attributed to lack of
background knowledge by most customers, and
the need for restaurants to adopt production-line
methods.
Chinese Food (1972)

DANISH FOOD

Astrid Slebsager
May is the season of small fjord shrimps . . . and
the first new potatoes . . . grown in the sandy soil
on the island of Samsø in the Kattegat . . . are
always the first Danish new potatoes on the
market . . .
Cooking with the Danes (1978)

Nika Hazleton
. . . incredible Danish fancy desserts are embel-
lished like an eighteenth-century lady-in-waiting
out to tempt the king. They tempt the diner
beyond endurance and he yields with a 'never
mind, never mind', as he takes his shameless third

helping ... To deprive a Dane of his boiled potatoes would be as cruel as depriving a baby of his bottle.

Danish Cooking (1967)

Linda Wolfe (ed.)

In Denmark, the word ... *smørrebrød* means bread and butter ... and may have begun with the Viking custom of using flat bread as a plate, upon which to eat other foods.

McCall's Introduction to Scandinavian Cooking (1960)

DUTCH FOOD

Jan Morgan

It might at first seem a little far-fetched to say that the bicycle has probably had as much influence on the Dutch cuisine as anything else ... Dutch food is substantial, simple and straightforward — nothing creates more of an appetite than cycling along an open road against the wind and rain!

From Holland With Love (1979)

Carol Willson and John Goode

A colleague predicted we would enjoy Scandinavia because, as in Japan, we would be able to eat raw fish again. Yet it was much farther south, at Marken on the shores of Ijsselmeer (that we once knew as Zuyder Zee) that raw herring with onions was offered as a snack at afternoon teatime.

'If It's Herring, This Must be Holland', *Financial Review* (1985)

ENGLISH COOKING

Frank Harris
1855-1931

... the English ideal of cooking is the best in the world; it is the aristocratic ideal and consists in the desire to give each article of food its own especial flavour ...

The drawback ... [is] that England has scarcely any cooks, and so it is seldom you find their ideals carried out.

My Life and Loves

'Cassandra' [William Connor]	The British do really WANT bad, coarse food ... Millions of young men, battle-trained on hasty NAAFI cooking, have come to worship [egg on chips] in which the egg is usually burnt or seized-up in a yellow, stodgy mess. The chips are soused in cottonseed oil, with the blackened portions carefully retained to preserve the much-appreciated flavour of rottenness.

'King Hal's Pie', *Daily Mirror* (1955)

GERMAN FOOD

Heinrich Heine 1797-1856	Food in Hamburg is divine. Indeed, one finds dishes here which our philosophers know nothing about.

Cited in 'City Meals in Old Hamburg', *Stroll Through Old Hamburg* (1981)

Carol Willson and John Goode	In summer, the squares [of Bonn] sprout sidewalk cafes like mushrooms, and at adjoining shops you can choose from 50 different local sausages, or settle for a few slices of superb ham. For a more formal meal, try 'Em Hottsche', just beside the Rathaus ... You can get a hearty meal of soup and main course for only $A6. Venison, local mushrooms and a berry sauce will cost $12.

'Where Seven Giants Carved the Mountains', *Sun-Herald* (1984)

GREEK COOKING

Chrissa Paradissis	Greek cuisine is ... the original cuisine, and it was the Turks, Italians and Europeans who actually borrowed from the Greeks whenever they came in contact with them ... the 2500-year-old Ancient Hellenic Cuisine was adopted and adapted by Rome and the rest of Italy. The Byzantine aristocrats adhered to the dictates of the Hellenistic Cuisine ... The Turks, in turn, adopted the mediaeval [Byzantine] Greek Cuisine, naming these borrowed recipes in their own Turkish language [to be] passed on to Greeks under Turkish rule.

The Best Book of Greek Cookery (1979)

Theresa Karas Yianilos

Greek cooks learned to add great amounts of garlic to meat and vegetables, to please the Turkish palate. The famous Greek dish of *Moussaka* was born when the Arabs [Turks] introduced the ... eggplant. Greeks shared the same delight as the Turks over the hot beverage made from coffee beans some Arab discovered growing in Ethiopia ... the Turkish habit of nibbling sweetmeats at all hours was contagious ... When the Turks were finally driven out of Greece in 1821 ... they left behind a new flavour in Greek cooking.

The Complete Greek Cookbook (1970)

HUNGARIAN COOKING

Anonymous

... the secret of Hungarian cuisine: 'Its sweet onion, noble paprika, unmatched bacon, the very best sour cream and a thousand years of experience.'

Anonymous 20th century restaurateur, cited by G. Lang in *The Cuisine of Hungary* (1971)

HUNGARIAN FOOD

Ann Bridge

... the chief impression after a year of Hungarian food ... is not of paprika but of raspberries ... large, firm, aromatic — and one ate them in delicious circumstances.

Food in Three Continents

Carol Willson and John Goode

... what better conclusion to such an exciting excursion [to the Bugacpuszta] than a meal at the Bugac Csarda, a splendidly rustic restaurant ... a meal will probably consist of *gulyas* [goulash] soup, a meal in itself; but leave some room for the home-grown pork and vegetables that follow. Then, if you've any more space, try to conclude your meal with the traditional pancake, filled with apricot purée and flamed with *korte palinka*, the local apricot *eau de vie*.

'Puszta: Land of Wine, Music and Horsemen', *Sun-Herald* (1986)

248

ITALY AND ITALIANS

Matthew Prior
1664-1721

Salad, and eggs, and lighter fare,
Tune the Italian spark's guitar.
Alma

M. Lapolla

Italian dishes . . . are different from the usual English fare. The everyday dishes are simple . . . more festive ones are perhaps ornate.
Good Food From Italy (1954)

Anonymous

Cooking in Italy . . . consists of serving something exquisitely fresh, with the least amount of modification in the process of preparation.
Cited in *The Tuscan Cookbook* (1979)

Hilaire Belloc
1870-1953

. . . In Italy, the traveller notes
With great disgust the flesh of goats
Appearing on the table d'hotes;
And even this the natives spoil
By frying it in rancid oil.
On Food

JAPANESE COOKING

Andrew Wong

Head chef Masa (of the Shin Ju Japanese restaurant in Sydney) is candid in his appraisal of all Australian seafood. 'Everything tastes better in Japan. It is something to do with the way it is cooked. We do it with love.'
'Faced With Competition, Our Oysters Fall Apart', *The Weekend Australian* (1984)

Carol Willson and John Goode

Traditional Japanese cooking . . . is far more than a means of satisfying an appetite. It is inextricably mixed with aesthetics, religion, tradition and history. It has a symbolism that would take a westerner a lifetime to learn, and yet partaking of it is a divine adventure.
'Eating in Japan . . . a Divine Adventure', *Epicurean* (1982)

Ian McQueen

. . . the Japanese do eat raw fish (sashimi) . . . If it seems a strange practice, remember how Westerners eat oysters. Sashimi has a weak flavour, with no 'fishy' taste or smell . . . [raw fish with rice] is very tasty . . .

Japan — a Travel Survival Kit (1981)

MALAYSIAN AND NONYA FOOD

Lee Sook Ching

. . . a delightful and fascinating blend of the best of Malay, Chinese, Indian, Thai and European cuisine.

Cook Malaysian (1982)

Kenneth Mitchell

The predominant religions [of Malaysia] are Islam, Buddhism and Hinduism . . . in a Muslim diet, pork is strictly forbidden and so the majority of Malay dishes tend to be of beef. However, beef is never eaten by the Hindu . . . and pork remains the favourite meat of the Chinese . . .

A Taste of Malaysia (1980)

Mrs Lee Chin Koon

Straits-born Chinese . . . ladies are called 'Nonyas' . . . Nonya food is so complicated that it takes years to learn and master . . . Nonya recipes are usually hot and spicy and call for the use of a lot of pungent roots, aromatic leaves and other ingredients such as candlenuts, shallots, shrimp paste and, of course, chillies. Sometimes lemon, lime, tamarind, *blimbing* and green mangoes are used to give certain recipes a sharp, sour flavour . . . Many of our dishes have Indonesian origins . . . We Nonyas seldom eat fruit, but finish our meal with cakes made from glutinous rice and coconut milk. We also drink lots of coffee . . . in this we follow the Malay custom.

Mrs Lee's Cookbook (1974)

Charmaine Solomon

Nonya style of food — a mixture of Chinese ingredients and Malay spices, cooked in a way that is the perfect mingling of the two cultures . . . Most recipes are based on a *rempah* — a paste of various spices . . . pounded to just the right degree with a stone mortar and pestle. The pounding itself is an art that must be mastered. Too little and the paste will not be smooth enough, too much and it will become too liquid.

The Complete Asian Cookbook (1976)

MEXICANA

Charles H. Baker Jr We . . . can affirm that our Yucatan most certainly ripped the bud out of his *Agave Americana* and drank the fermented *pulque* — a fluid which tastes faintly like mildewed donkeys — centuries before Montezuma's parents journeyed southward to the Valley of Cortez.

The Gentleman's Companion (1946)

Note: *pulque*, the highly potent fermented juice of the agave — or maguey — plant. Tequila and Mescal, which taste quite different from one another, are distilled from agave juice. J.G.

Craig Clairborne Long ago, [Diana Kennedy] and I agreed on the merits of Mexican food. It is, we decided, earthy food, festive food, happy food, celebration food. It is, in short, peasant food raised to the level of high and sophisticated art.

Foreword to *The Cuisine of Mexico* (1972)

Diana Kennedy . . . far too many people know Mexican food as a 'mixed plate': a crisp taco filled with ground meat, heavily flavoured with an all-purpose chilli powder; a soggy *tamal*, covered with a sauce that turns up on everything — too sweet and too over-poweringly onioned — a few fried beans and something else that looks and tastes like all the rest. Where is the wonderful play of texture, colour, and flavour that makes up an authentic well-cooked Mexican meal?

The Cuisine of Mexico (1972)

PORTUGUESE FOOD

William Beckford The Portuguese had need have the stomach of ostriches to digest the loads of greasy victuals with which they cram themselves. Their vegetables, their rice, their poultry are all stewed in the

251

essence of ham and so strongly seasoned with pepper and spices that a spoonful of pease . . . is sufficient to set one's mouth in a flame.

Italy: with Sketches of Spain and Portugal (18th century)

Quentin Crewe Portuguese cookery, with its dismal quality, is not helped by generations of poverty.

Quentin Crewe's International Pocket Food Book (1980)

SCOTTISH FOOD

Hugh
MacDiarmid
1892-1978

You canna gang to a Burns supper even
Wi'oot some wizened scrunt o'a knock-knee
Chinee turns roon to say, 'Him Haggis—velly
    goot!'
And ten to wan the piper is a cockney.

A Drunk Man Looks at the Thistle

SPAIN

Hillaire Belloc
1870-1953

The Spaniard, I have heard it said
Eats garlic, by itself, on bread . . .

On Food

Anna
MacMiadhachain

Whatever one might think about the smells involved, the fish markets of Spain are . . . visually exciting places.

Spanish Regional Cookery (1976)

Quentin Crewe On the whole, beef . . . is not worth eating. Unless . . . for the hell of it, you want to go to a restaurant in a bull-fighting town . . . where you can eat through some six to eight courses, ranging from brains . . . [and] testicles . . . to cutlets and steaks.

'Spain: Meat and Poultry', *Quentin Crewe's*
International Pocket Food Book (1980)

THAI FOOD

M. L. Taw Kritakara and Pimsai Amranand

When one is asked to describe Thai food, one usually says 'It's hot, chilli hot' . . . the basic characteristic taste of Thai food . . . comes from a mixture of salt, pepper, garlic and coriander root pounded together. It is this aromatic combination that turns fried pork or chicken into Thai fried pork . . . as opposed to Chinese fried pork or American fried chicken.

Modern Thai Cooking (1977)

CHEF'S SECRETS

Charpentier

After Baron Rothschild asked for a sauce recipe: 'Baron', Camous retorted haughtily, 'it will never be too inconvenient an hour of the day for me to duplicate it for you; but Monsieur le Baron, this is my treasure vault you would invade.' Jean tapped his head with such vigour as to sound as if he were rapping on a table than his skull.

Those Rich and Great Ones (1935)

COOKERY BOOKS AND THEIR WRITERS

Reay Tannahill

. . . father of all Greek cookery-writers . . . the inventor of 'made' dishes, was Archestratus who, in the fourth century B.C., quartered the known world in search of information on food and drink.

The Fine Art of Food (1968)

In 1375, the first cookery book of modern times . . . [was] compiled by Guillaume Tirel, 'first squire of the kitchen' to Charles VI of France . . . written under the pseudonym of Taillevent . . . [It] is very tempting to take the word in its literal sense of 'cut-wind', for the mediaeval digestive system was much afflicted by wind, and any author who offered the promise of reducing it would have been a popular man . . . *Le Viandier*, as the book is known . . . holds out little hope [for such a cure].

Ibid.

The first printed cookery book came ... from Renaissance Italy in 1475. It was written ... by the Vatican Librarian ... Bartolomeo de Sacchi ... known as Platina. His book, *De Honesta Voluptate*, was partly a cookery book and partly a guide to good health.

Ibid.

Peter Wynne *Le Managier de Paris* ... written about 1393 by an elderly gentleman as a book on housekeeping for his young bride ... [A] cookbook compiled in 1390 by the chefs of Richard II ... was edited and published in 1780 by ... Samuel Pegge under the title *The Forme of Cury*.

Apples (1975)

Andre Simon *The Forme of Cury*, the 'Mrs. Beeton's' of the fifteenth and sixteenth centuries in England...

'From Esau to Escoffier', *We Shall Eat and Drink Again* (c.1943)

Laurens van der Post Once there was not a city or town of any importance in the old British Africa which was without a mission book-shop containing cookery books written by missionary ladies for the guidance of African housewives ... a mixture of the authors' nostalgia for their own native foods and their desires to give Africans a more balanced diet. The emphasis was obviously not on taste so much as on the health...

First Catch Your Eland (1977)

J. C. Furnas Books which suggest simplicity in the kitchen never sell well.

Man, Bread and Destiny (1937)

INDEX OF TOPICS